SHARON K SOLOMON

The Pencil That Wouldn't Die

*First published by AimHi Press 2020*

*Copyright © 2020 by Sharon K Solomon*

*All rights reserved. No part of this publication may be reproduced, stored or transmitted in any form or by any means, electronic, mechanical, photocopying, recording, scanning, or otherwise without written permission from the publisher. It is illegal to copy this book, post it to a website, or distribute it by any other means without permission.*

*This novel is entirely a work of fiction. The names, characters and incidents portrayed in it are the work of the author's imagination. Any resemblance to actual persons, living or dead, events or localities is entirely coincidental.*

*Names: Solomon, Sharon. | Traynor, Daniel, Illustrations.*

*Title: The Pencil That Wouldn't Die / by Sharon Solomon*

*Description: Orlando, FL | AimHi Press, 2020. | Summary: Middle school is already so hard, but when summer comes along for twins Sam and Abby, the problems don't end. Will a pencil turn a boring summer into a scientific adventure?*

*Identifiers: Library of Congress Control Number: 2020938200 (print) | ISBN 978-1-945493-26-3 (paperback)*

*Subjects: CYAC: Middle school. | Science. | Mystery. | Adventure. | Club. |*

*Classification: LCC PZ7.1.S65 Pen 2020(print)*

*LC record available at https://lccn.loc.gov/2020938200*

*First edition*

*ISBN: 978-1-945493-26-3*

*This book was professionally typeset on Reedsy. Find out more at reedsy.com*

# Jackson City Map

# Chapter One

As Sam and Abby Jackson began their summer vacation, they weren't expecting anything exciting to happen. But that would soon change. Every year it was the same old thing. Mom said, "Clean your rooms. Everything off the floor." So the ten-year-old twins did. Sam got a couple of trash bags, threw his stuff in, and tossed them in his closet. Abby jammed her things into her drawers and told her mom she was finished.

"That was hard work for our first day off," Abby said at lunch. She smiled and focused her green eyes on her mom.

"I found my hamster crawling under my bed. Germie's back in his cage. I even cleaned it out." Sam said, thinking Abby was trying to smile her way out of it as she usually did.

Mom nodded and handed them bottles of lemonade. "So what're you two planning for this summer besides swimming?"

Sam preferred soda, but Mom said lemonade was healthier and better at quenching thirst. He suspected it was also her way to help him lose weight since he did have a problem with that. He envied Abby, his twin, who was far more athletic and slimmer.

"Not much happens in Jackson City," Abby said. "I need a scout project, though. Maybe I can dig up some information on great-grandpa Joseph Jackson and make a scout history project out of it. So far, I only know he had a farm and a paper mill and that our town is named after him."

"That would be a good project," Mom said. "Sam, what about you? Don't you need a project for your badge too?"

Sam piped up, "I haven't a clue." Just as long as I'm not near Joey Gordon, it'll be fine, he thought, wondering why the son of his scout leader always had to mess with him when nobody was around.

"Sam," Mom said, "why didn't you tell Dad and me? We can help you find a project."

"You woulda just said solve it yourself. That's your favorite phrase."

And it was. When Abby lost her soccer cleats, Mom just told her to look harder. When Sam couldn't find Germie, their mom patted him on the back and told him she knew Germie was around somewhere. So the twins were used to solving their own problems.

"Well, I'm sure you'll come up with something cool," Mom said and placed their lunch on the table. "I have confidence in both of you."

"Oh, no," Sam said when he saw a plate of crunchy carrots and celery. "Are you trying to starve me?"

Abby smiled. "Veggies are good for us," she said, eyeing the carrot as if it was her favorite piece of candy.

"No worries, I also made egg salad sandwiches for you, Sam," Mom said.

Sam, munched on crunchy carrots and celery along with an egg salad sandwich. That was when the excitement began.

Mom opened her lemonade bottle. "Hey, there are fun facts on the lemonade lids. Listen to this one. Polar bears can smell things twenty miles away."

Sam laughed. "I wouldn't want to smell someone's body odor even twenty miles away, but that's cool, Mom."

Abby said, "I have one too. The only insect that can turn its head is a praying mantis. Is that true? Hmm, who knew?"

Sam pulled open his bottle. "My turn. The average lead pencil can draw a line thirty-five miles long." He reread it and laughed. "No way! How could one pencil possibly do that?"

Mom said, "It must be true if they put it on the lid like that."

Sam put the lid on the table. "Thirty-five miles? A pencil can't write that long."

Mom looked thoughtful. "Thirty-five miles is a long distance. It's a half-mile from here to Grandma's house, so it's a mile both ways. Multiply that by thirty-five and you're in business."

# CHAPTER ONE

Abby said, "I'm with Sam. I don't think it's possible."

Sam picked up the lid again. "You know, I need a science project for a scout badge. Maybe this will work," Sam said.

"What will?" Abby asked.

Sam turned the lid over in his hand. "If I can prove this is impossible, that could be my science project."

Abby's face lit up. "Can I help? I need to earn a Junior Girl Scout badge."

Sam mumbled. "I thought you were gonna do a history project on the Jackson family."

"Well, your pencil thingy sounds more interesting."

Sam saw his mother looking at him.

Abby said, "What's the matter? You don't want to work with me?" .

Mom glared at Sam.

Sam sighed. "Oh, all right. After lunch, let's go over to the Gordons and ask if this will work as MY project. You can help"

Sam sipped at his lemonade. He was excited about getting his scout badge with such a fun experiment but thinking how he didn't want to start his summer working with his twin sister. While he liked having a sister, her being a twin sometimes made life difficult.

Mom smiled, "Maybe you could ask that nice Gordon kid, Joseph, to work with you on this."

"I like Joey," Abby piped up. "He has freckles and a cute smile like me."

Sam shivered. He'd almost forgotten about Joey Gordon, the bully.

# Chapter Two

The twins scarfed down their lunch and headed across the street to the Gordons. Joey was the oldest of their five kids, and was going into sixth grade, like Sam.

"Just let me do the talking," Sam said, hoping Joey wasn't home.

Abby wondered why her brother seemed so nervous.

He hesitated and then rang the bell. He thought, what if Joey answered.

Abby straightened her shirt.

Mr. Gordon answered. "Well, if it isn't the Jackson duo. How's your first day of summer vacation going?"

"Pretty good," Abby said, aiming her smile at him.

Sam peered into the room. The other Gordon kids were on the floor playing, but no sign of Joey.

Mr. Gordon invited them inside. "So what brings you here?"

Sam showed him the lemonade lid. "Can I earn a science badge trying to prove this? I mean, it's impossible for a pencil to last for 35 miles, don't ya think?"

Mr. Gordon read the lid . "Interesting. I always thought of you as a kind of mad scientist, Sam." He smiled. "Okay. I'm curious myself if this is true. If you write down everything you do and show your proof… why not, Buddy? I think this could be fun. It's definitely a challenge. Sure. Go for it."

That's when Abby put in her two cents. She didn't like being left out. "Excuse me, Mr. Gordon. Is Mrs. Gordon around?"

Sam frowned. He knew Abby staying quiet was too good to last.

Mr. Gordon called for his wife, "Honey, the Jackson twins are here."

## CHAPTER TWO

Mrs. Gordon pushed through the swinging kitchen door with pink icing on her cheek and a crying baby in her arms. "Oh, hi, Abby. I was just frosting Rosie's birthday cake."

Abby spoke loudly so Mrs. Gordon could hear her over the howling baby. "Sam's gonna earn a science badge for proving whether a pencil can write a line for thirty-five miles. Is there a way I can earn a Junior Badge for working on this too?"

Sam shuffled his feet and looked annoyed.

Mrs. Gordon bounced Rosie in her arms. "You want to test whether a pencil can write 35 miles?" She looked thoughtful. "Well, let's see. There is a Junior Fitness Badge. This sounds like it could be an interesting challenge. Maybe you could help Sam by biking around town with the pencil and keeping track of your mileage."

Mr. Gordon nodded. "Sam can ride his bike with you and get his fitness badge, too."

Sam's frown gave him away. He didn't love the idea of having to ride his bicycle 35 miles anytime, let alone during the summer.

But then Mr. Gordon said, "Wow! You two can be a Mad Scientist team. You can figure out how to do the pencil part and the biking to earn your science and fitness badges at the same time."

"Cool," Abby said, giving Sam a triumphant smile.

Sam sighed. Could this get any worse?

Hefting Rosie on her shoulder, Mrs. Gordon said, "Gotta go. Benjy's up from his nap. Good luck you two. It will be fun for you working together like this."

Walking across the street to their old farmhouse, Sam growled, "What're you grinning about, Abigail Jackson?"

"I'm excited to have a summer project with you, Sam. It will be so fun."

Sam mumbled, "You know I hate to exercise. Sweating isn't my thing. Now I gotta work with you and sweat. Oh brother! This is going to be some summer."

Abby's smile turned into a frown.

I don't see how this can get worse, Sam thought.

That was when Joey Gordon appeared in the yard with his friend Owen Parker. "I guess you need your sister to walk you across the street, Jackson," he taunted.

Abby turned and looked like she was gonna snap back an answer but Sam said in a low voice, " Ignore him. If we act like he's invisible, maybe he'll disappear."

As they walked to their house, Abby realized Sam was really afraid of Joey Gordon and wondered if there was something she could do to help.

# Chapter Three

**A**bby was still thinking about Joey when Sam sat down on the porch rocking chair. "I need to get to work on my science project right away. I hope I didn't bite off more than I can chew."

Abby wondered why he kept saying it was his project, but decided to not argue with him yet about that.

Sam said, "The math and science part will be a cinch." He looked at Abby. "Why'd you bring up that bike part? I'm not crazy about biking around Jackson City, especially not in the summer heat."

"Well, the biking part will be easy-peasy for me, but not the math part," Abby said "Maybe we'll both learn something new. Who knows, I could turn into a mad scientist like you and Dad—"

"Well, I'm not gonna be a star soccer player like you. But I guess a little exercise won't kill me," said Sam. Just then a light bulb lit up in his head. "I just got an idea, Abby. I need to check something on my computer right away."

Sam rushed upstairs and got out his laptop. He typed in *ways to measure miles.*

*Abby watched over Sam's shoulder. Usually, Sam shooed her from his room, but this time he was too busy working on their project. She stared at the screen as* up popped the words, *odometer, speedometer,* and *pedometer.*

"Hey, Abby, you gotta see this," Sam said.

Abby asked, "What are these things?"

Sam pointed. "These are all things I can use to measure distances for my project.".

"Our project," Abby said.

Sam looked at her and sighed. "Anyway, if we're gonna earn scout badges, we have to measure our distance when we bike around town."

"Gotcha, but how will these help us?"

Sam pointed to the computer screen. "These are three tools to measure distances. The question is which one can I...we use?"

Abby read the definitions on the screen:

*odometer – an instrument that measures distance traveled by a vehicle*

*pedometer – an instrument that measures distance by the number of steps a person takes as in walking*

*speedometer – a devise in a motor vehicle that measures speed*

"We're too young to drive a car, so nix on the speedometer," Abby said. .

"And there's no way I'm gonna walk thirty-five miles," Sam said.. "So the only one that might work is the odometer." He quickly typed in the name of the local hardware store on the search screen and then typed in odometer. "Abby, the prices on the internet to buy one start at thirty dollars!" He looked at her. "I don't have that much. It looks like we've got to figure out something else. You and your fitness badge!"

Abby was still studying the screen. "Odd-meter? Doesn't my new bike have one? It came with lots of gadgets and gizmos."

Sam corrected her that it was not pronounced, Odd-meter, but called an o-dom-met-er."

"Whatever," Abby said. "But I think I have one on my bike."

Sam followed Abby to the garage. And when they went to look at her bike, it did have an odometer. "You're right," Sam said. "That is an odometer."

"I told you so," Abby said.

Sam groaned. He hated when anyone said, "I told you so," but at least, she had the odometer he needed. " Lucky you, Abby, that you outgrew your old bike before I did. I'm still riding my old one. Mom and Dad promised me a new bike for our birthday in October." He hoped they'd keep their promise, but knew money was tight this year. "Let's tell Mom about our project," he said and walked toward the house.

Abby smiled. Sam had called it 'their' project.

# CHAPTER THREE

Mom was outside planting flowers when Abby rushed up and said, "Guess what! My new bike has an odd-meter! We're gonna use it to track our miles on our bikes. We have to for our scout fitness badges."

"A what?" Mom looked up.

Sam got right in Abby's face and shouted. "Odometer! Not odd-meter. How many times do I have to tell you?"

Abby looked shocked.

Mom stood up and glared at Sam.

"Sorry," Sam mumbled, realizing Mom was glaring at him with the look you get before you're grounded.

Mom nodded and put her arm on Abby's shoulder. "Now, what's this all about?" she asked.

Sam knew he had to calm down. "Mr. and Mrs. Gordon liked the pencil experiment."

"You mean the one where the pencil will last…how many miles?"

"Thirty-five," Abby said. "We're both getting our fitness badges too. We're going to ride our bikes 35 miles."

Mom looked at Sam. "You're going to ride your bike 35 miles?"

Sam nodded. "With Abby's odometer, measuring our thirty-five miles around Jackson City will be ….."

"Easy-peasy," Abby finished the sentence.

Sam sighed.

Mom asked, "What about the pencil part ?"

"Oh, right, the pencil," Sam shrugged. "I almost forgot about that."

"Me too," Abby said.

"I'll have to figure out a way to attach the pencil to my bicycle," Sam said, picturing his bike and wondering how he could do that.

Mom gave Sam a warm smile. She brushed dirt off her knees and gathered her gardening tools. "Sleep on it, you two," she said.

Besides 'Work it out yourself', their mom's other favorite expression was, 'Sleep on it'.

"Sleeping on a pencil sounds uncomfortable. Come on, Sam., let's go sleep on it." Abby laughed.

Sam shook his head, but had to laugh at his sister's sense of humor. "How can we sleep on it? It's only four o'clock." He followed Abby to the porch. It had been a long first day of vacation and it was only half over! This project was not going to be as easy as he thought. How am I going to attach a pencil to my bike?

The twins sat on the front porch steps, lost in thought. When Sam spied Joey Gordon crossing the street, he stood up quickly. "Let's go inside," he muttered, pulling open the screen door.

Abby wondered if her brother would ever get the guts to face his fear.

# Chapter Four

On day two of summer vacation, Sam and Abby enjoyed their favorite breakfast, blueberry pancakes. Sam drowned his in syrup. Abby put a thin coating of syrup on her stack.

"So, did you solve your problem?" Mom asked as she poured Sam a glass of chocolate milk.

"Well, I slept on it, and have some ideas for earning our badges," Sam said between juicy bites of pancakes. "What if I tied a pencil to the kickstand of my bike? Then we could ride around Jackson City and see if that works to prove what the lid said."

Abby nodded. "Tying it to my kickstand would be better. I ride better than you."

"My bike," Sam said. "I came up with this experiment."

Abby sighed. "Whatever."

Sam laid out a map of Jackson City on the table. "Thirty-five miles is far. I figure we can ride to different places in town and keep track of our miles."

"Then we could see how long the pencil lasts," Abby said. "I've got a small spiral notebook we can use. "I'll ride behind you and sharpen the pencil when it gets low."

Sam looked surprised. Maybe Abby would be of help after all.

Abby walked to her room and returned with a small red pencil sharpener. She put it in her jeans pocket. "I'm ready. Let's ride to the movie theatre and back. It'll be both exercise and science!"

Mom had been listening silently, glad her twins appeared to be working together on this project. "You just be careful. Okay? Always remember, safety first."

Sam nodded.

"And Sam, take care of your sister," Mom added, giving Abby a hug.

"I'll watch out for Sam, too," Abby said.

Sam was glad they were about to start this new adventure. "Abby, You're always so perky. Don't you ever get tired?" he asked.

Abby giggled. "Don't worry, Sam. I've got enough energy for both of us."

Sam didn't look thrilled but nodded his head. Mom had insisted they pack PBJ sandwiches and juice boxes into their backpacks. Sam also added his pen and Abby's notebook.

In the garage, Sam bent down over his bike. "Hold the pencil while I tie it to the kickstand," he ordered Abby.

Abby bent down and held the pencil. "Are you sure this is going to work?" she asked.

Sam ignored her as he tied a string around and around a brand new lead pencil and his kickstand. "That should hold it," he said, looking like a doctor admiring his completed operation. "Let's go!"

"Not yet. Remember the Girl Scouts motto, 'Be prepared'," Abby said, handing Sam a tube of sunblock and his floppy hat.

Sam looked at the floppy hat with disgust. "Did Mom give you those?"

Abby nodded.

By the time they strapped on their backpacks, and were finally ready to go, it was nearly ten o'clock and Sam was already sweating. "Maybe we should do this tomorrow," he said, wondering if he was up for a four mile ride on his bike.

Abby shook her head. "You can do it. No more stalling. Let's get those fitness badges now!"

Sam picked up his bike and adjusted the pencil so it hit the ground. Here we go, he thought, as he mounted the two-wheeler. "You stay behind me," he ordered Abby, as he started down the road.

Riding behind, Abby shouted, "I'll let you know when it's time to sharpen the pencil."

Sam was focusing on riding slowly enough for the pencil to stay on the road

## CHAPTER FOUR

surface. He kept looking at his kickstand so he didn't see what was ahead of him.

Joey Gordon was outside with his little sisters. "Hey, Lardo. Riding with your sister?" He let out a nasty laugh.

Sam pedaled faster. Joey's mean laugh echoed in his brain as he turned the corner onto Jackson Street. That darn Joey, he thought, glad his sister hadn't heard what the bully shouted at him.

Sam turned right on Hill Street and slowed down.

Abby saw he was huffing and puffing up the hill. When they turned onto Broad Street, Abby rode ahead of him. "Are you okay?" she shouted.

Sam gave her a dirty look as he tried to keep pedaling.

Abby doubled back and slowed her pace. She knew Sam was struggling. She noticed Sam's sweaty, tomato-red face, but didn't want to say anything that would upset him. Each time she saw the pencil was no longer touching the ground, she called, "Pencil stop!"

Sam pulled over and they parked their bikes.

Abby would sharpen the pencil, which she worried was getting shorter and shorter by the minute. There was no way it was going to last 35 miles at this rate.

Sam would retie the pencil and adjust it so it hit the ground, but he was worried, too. Something wasn't right.

Finally reaching the movie theatre parking lot, Abby suggested they stop for lunch. Not only was she worried about the pencil not lasting, but also about her brother.

"Great," Sam barked, "I'm starved. It's awful hot."

Abby hadn't broken a sweat. She thought, biking is a lot of work for someone who usually sits in front of a TV or computer, but kept her thoughts to herself.

Sam gobbled down his PBJ sandwich and his drink. I'll never make it, he thought, staring at Abby who never seemed to tire, sweat, or worry about anything.

After lunch, Sam almost fell asleep while resting under a tree.

Abby nudged him awake with her elbow. "There's a fountain. Let's splash some water on our faces," she said.

After they both were soaking wet, Abby got back on her bike. "Heading home should be easier," she said.

Sam groaned when he swung his leg over his bike. "I hope there's something left of the pencil," he said as he reluctantly began to pedal.

I hope there's something left of Sam, Abby thought, as she worried her overweight brother might not make it all the way home.

Abby stopped them six more times on the way home to sharpen the pencil and to give Sam a much-needed break.

By the time they reached the barn, the pencil was the size of a pinkie finger.

Sam looked exhausted as he examined the small pencil. "I don't get it," he said, worried his project was a failure before he even started.

Abby said, "My odd-meter says we went four miles. We did great."

Sam shook his head, but jotted down the date and the number four in the notebook. "It sure seemed further than that. Look at our pencil. There's hardly anything left. What did we do wrong?"

"Beats me." Abby shrugged and then smiled. "Let's sleep on it."

Sam wondered if sleep would make his aching body feel better, or solve the problem of why the pencil had hardly lasted four miles. It was supposed to last 35 miles! This is going to be some summer, he thought. He wondered what would happen if he just gave up on this crazy science and fitness project which was already killing him.

# Chapter Five

On day three of summer vacation, Abby woke Sam up. "It's after nine o'clock, Sam! Move it or lose it. We have lots to do."

Moaning, Sam sat up slowly and struggled to get into a T-shirt and shorts. As he crept downstairs, he winced at each step. "Every muscle of my body is screaming," he said as he fell into a chair.

"Well, Rip Van Winkle, did you sleep on it?" Abby asked. taking a bite of her yogurt, granola, and fruit.

Sam glared at her, "I want to know your secret. You're not the least bit tired from yesterday."

Abby shrugged. "I thought you did good for your first day," she said.

"Thanks." Sam munched on his bagel, egg and cheese sandwich. "Anyway, I think I know what went wrong yesterday."

Abby fixed her green eyes on her dark-haired, dark-eyed twin brother. "You mean why the pencil got so short?"

"You noticed? Yesterday, the pencil dragged on the cement sidewalks and blacktop streets. Can you read the lemonade lid again?"

Abby picked up the lid. "The average lead pencil can draw a line thirty-five miles long."

"Right, but it never said what to draw it on. A rough surface will wear the pencil out like that." Sam snapped his fingers.

Abby's eyebrows raised. "Do you think they meant writing on paper?"

"Yep. They must have."

"Great! Thirty-five miles of paper would fill up this house. That'd be awesome! "

Their dad overheard them. He was a math teacher at Jackson City High School. "Do you guys know how to measure a mile of paper?" he asked.

They shook their heads.

Dad walked over to the computer. "Okay, Sam, type in, *How long is a mile?*"

The answer popped up: *5,280 feet or 1,700 yards.*

Then their dad said, "If one sheet of paper is about a foot long, you'll need lots of paper."

Sam took out his calculator. "Wow! That would be 184,800 feet of paper."

Abby exclaimed. "That's a lot of paper. How can we do that?"

Dad said, "Sleep on it. I've confidence in you two. You'll figure it out."

Now Dad's doing it too? Sam sat and tried to picture 35 miles of paper.

So did Abby.

Suddenly, Sam shot up in his chair. "Abby, I've got it! If we make one mile of paper, we can draw on it thirty-five times."

Abby smiled. "You're a genius, Bro."

"Great idea!" Dad high-fived Sam. "I knew you could figure it out."

"Only one problem," Sam said.

"Only one?" Abby asked, thinking this project had already been a bunch of problems.

Sam looked at her. "Where can we get a mile of paper?"

Dad smiled. "You know I don't like interfering with my mad scientists, but your grandma has loads of paper.. They've been on her shelves for years."

Sam looked puzzled.

His father explained,"Your grandpa used lots of paper in his office. After he died, Grandma just kept the packages on a shelf."

"So," Abby said, "We'd actually be helping Grandma clean up! I'll bet there's even a badge for that."

Sam moaned. "Your fitness badge almost killed me yesterday," he said.

"Well, you better get ready to ride again. We're off to Grandma's house," Abby said, already racing for the garage.

Grandma's house was just five blocks straight down Jackson Street. Like the city, the street was named after their great-grandpa Joseph Jackson. He had a large farm and a paper mill that provided a lot of jobs until it closed

## CHAPTER FIVE

down.

The twins parked their bikes by Grandma's back door.

Sam was out of breath after chasing Abby on her bike. Would Grandma's stash of paper be enough for their experiment?

# Chapter Six

"Well, what a nice treat," Grandma said when she saw the twins by her door. "Just in time for snacks. She led them into her large, old-fashioned, kitchen.

Over a plate of chocolate chip cookies and glasses of milk, Sam and Abby shared their plans with Grandma.

"So, you're really going to try this experiment?" Grandma asked. "It sounds interesting, but a pencil being able to write 35 miles? I don't believe it."

"Neither do we," Sam said, "That's why we need to have some of Grandpa's paper."

Grandma sighed. "That was your Grandpa's old paper. I never got rid of anything after he passed away."

Sam had a feeling she wasn't going to give them the paper. He understood. "That's okay, Grandma."

Abby looked disappointed. "We really need a lot of paper," she said, aiming her eyes at her grandmother.

Grandma nodded. "Well, it's like your grandpa is helping you, in a way. Want me to drive the packages to your house?"

"Thank you, Grandma," Sam said, grateful that she wanted to help.

Abby added, "Now you and Grandpa are part of the Mad Scientist Team, too."

"He would have liked that," Grandma said and led them to the old office and the packages of paper.

When Sam saw all the packages of paper, he realized this was going to be more work. He looked at Abby and was glad she was here to help.

# CHAPTER SIX

After loading the paper into their Grandma's trunk, Sam and Abby biked behind Grandma's car.

Sam was so happy, that he thought nothing else could go wrong.

You-Know-Who was out front, but said nothing when he recognized Grandma's car. He shot Sam a dirty look.

Sam kept pedaling, acting as if Joey was invisible.

Abby shot Joey a dirty look back, but kept going. This was one problem Sam would have to take care of himself, she thought. Arriving at the barn, she announced, "My odd-meter says one mile. Yesterday we went four miles, so that's a total of five miles so far. Pretty good. Huh?"

Sam wrote in his notebook, deciding to ignore the annoying odd-meter part. Didn't Abby know any better or was she just trying to push his buttons? In either case, Sam decided not to correct her.

"I'm going to the house to say hi to your mother," Grandma said. "You two can unload the car."

Sam and Abby unloaded one stack of paper at a time.

"This could take forever," Sam said. "Let's put them in the wagon." Their house used to be Great-grandfather Joseph's farmhouse and Sam remembered the small red wagon he'd had as a child was stored in the old barn

They headed toward the huge barn in back of the house.

"I don't like going in here," Abby said. "There are bats."

Sam was surprised Abby was afraid of anything. "Bats are good for nature," he said. "Come on. I'll go in first." He pulled open the barn door and walked in. "See, nothing to be afraid of."

Abby wondered why if he was so brave now with bats, he couldn't be that brave with Joey Gordon.

"Got it," Sam said, pulling the wagon out of the barn. "The wheels are wobbly, but it should help."

Sam made moaning-groaning noises as he and Abby loaded and unloaded the wagon. It took three trips to the barn before the car was empty.

"Too bad this paper-lifting isn't part of my fitness badge," Abby said.

Grandma peeked her head inside the barn. "Good job! You emptied the car. I see you used your noodle and got out the old wagon. Good thinking. Well,

I'll be going home now. You two are quite a team."

Sam stared at the huge stacks of paper. "Well, now that we have all this paper, how are we going to attach the sheets together to make up a mile?" He sat on the dirt floor. "I wish I'd thought of all this before we started this darn thing."

"Can we use a stapler?" Abby asked.

Sam looked at his sister as if she was crazy. "Are you serious? Do you know how long it would take us to staple all this paper?"

Abby nodded her head. "We could tape it."

Sam said, "Where on earth can we get that much tape?"

Abby smiled. "We have loads of masking tape left over from my last scout project."

"We're gonna need it," Sam said.

Abby looked at the door. She'd heard someone or something by the door. She got up to investigate. "Who's here?" she asked.

Joey Gordon popped out from behind a bush. He peered into the barn. "Not biking today? Too much for you, Jackson?"

Sam's face turned red as a strawberry, but he stood up straight and aimed his chocolate-brown eyes on the bully. "Beat it, Gordon. We're busy."

"Gonna make me?" Joey snickered.

Sam stepped closer. It looked like they were going to fight, but Joey stepped back. "When you don't have your sister here to protect you, then you'll see. " He turned on his heel and left, laughing rudely as he walked away from the barn.

Abby raised her hand to high-five her brother. "Way to go, Bro! You stood up to him. It's about time."

Sam didn't raise his hand in a high-five. He was wondering if he would have fought with Joey. Did he really have the guts to face his bully?

Abby dropped her hand. "What's with you and Joey anyway?"

Sam looked at his sister and said, "He's been on me for years."

"Why? What does he have against you?"

Sam let out a deep breath. "Let's get back to work. We have to tape 5,280 sheets of paper together."

## CHAPTER SIX

Abby wanted to help her brother deal with his biggest problem, Joey Gordon, but Sam wasn't ready. "I'm not so great in math. How many packages is that?" she asked.

Sam, the human calculator figured it out. "Well, ten times five hundred equals five thousand. So we need ten and a half packages of paper."

"That doesn't sound so bad." Abby counted the packages on the barn floor by two's, "Two, four, six, eight, ten, twelve. We have enough!" She clapped her hands. "We should be done in no time."

Sam stared at the piles of paper. To him, they looked like a mountain. "I hope you're right," he muttered.

They each took a package of paper to opposite sides of the barn and began taping.

Two hours later, when Dad stuck his head in the barn door, he couldn't stop laughing. "Sam, you've got pieces of tape stuck all over you. And Abby, is that a new hairstyle?"

Abby mussed up her blond hair and pulled out a few pieces of masking tape. " My fingers are numb."

"My eyes are blurry," Sam said as he pushed himself up off the barn floor.

"How much did we get done? We must be almost finished," Abby said.

Sam looked at the half empty reams of paper. "I'd say about 250 sheets each."

"That's all?" Abby looked at her Sam. "This is going to take forever," she said.

Their father smiled. "You two need a break."

Sam replied. "Break? Dad, we just got started."

Just then, Mom called them for dinner.

Dad placed his hand on Sam's shoulder. "Sometimes, when you have a big job, you need to take breaks to give yourself time to get back into shape." He looked at Abby. "You two have done a lot already, but it's dinner time. Now, clean up and you'll feel better later." He mussed Sam's hair and left the barn.

Abby said, "Sam, Dad's right. We'll finish later."

Sam looked at the sheets of paper. "Okay. Let's roll it up."

They quickly rolled their taped pages into a large scroll.

"I deserve a fitness badge for this," Abby muttered. She held up her sore hands.

Sam replied, "I won't get my science badge 'til we finish the pencil experiment."

"Do you really think one pencil can last 35 miles?" Abby asked.

Sam shrugged. "I don't know, but if we show our proof, even if the pencil doesn't last, Mr. G has to give me the badge."

If we ever finish this, Abby thought, wondering if she was stupid to get involved in such a crazy project.

# Chapter Seven

Day four of summer vacation began with Abby eating a bowl of cereal, milk and a sliced banana.

Sam gobbled up a stack of pancakes dripping in butter and syrup. "You should eat healthier," Abby said. "You'd feel better."

Sam's body ached all over but he didn't dare tell that to Abby. What he really wanted was a day off. "I like what I like," he replied, drinking two glasses of chocolate milk with two chocolate donuts. He dreaded going back to taping the endless sheets of paper, but knew Abby was ready to run as usual.

But today was different. Abby sighed and said, "Sam, I need a break from paper taping. Look at the cuts on my fingers." She held up her hands.

Sam laughed and showed her his. They each had band aids wrapped around several of their fingers.."Abby," Sam said, "you're really disappointing me. I was so eager to get back to the barn and work." He was faking it. The last thing he wanted to do was face that huge pile of paper again.

Abby stared at her brother and then burst out laughing. "Sure, you do."

"Not!" Sam laughed.

Abby sighed. "But I need to get that fitness badge, and so do you."

Sam nodded. " Maybe we should ride our bikes in the mornings, before it gets real hot, and paper tape in the afternoons. OK?"

"Sure," Abby said. "Let's ride over to Jackson City Library today. I can pick up some good books."

"Great idea." Sam patted himself on the back as he walked to the barn. Well, she fell for that, he thought. Maybe working with his sister wouldn't be so bad after all.

In the barn, Sam grunted at the sight of the packages of paper. For once, he was eager to get their bikes and helmets.

Pedaling up Hill Street still made Sam sweat , but he made it to the library a little behind Abby who was sitting on a bench outside the library.

Sam's shirt was sticking to him from sweat, like bubble gum. I hate riding my bike, he thought, glad to sit on the bench.

"You're getting better at riding," Abby said. "She handed him a juice box and three chocolate chip cookies their Mom had packed for him. She unwrapped her two oatmeal raisin cookies and sipped slowly at her juice, making it last.

Sam finished his juice in a few gulps and his cookies were gone in two bites. "I wish I had more," he said, eyeing Abby's cookie.

Abby handed him her last oatmeal raisin cookie. "Here. You can have one of my snacks."

"Oatmeal? I don't know if I like those." He tasted it. "Not as bad as I thought. Thanks." He ate it up and felt thirsty again. "Any more drinks in your backpack?"

Abby pointed to the water fountain. "Water is good for you."

Sam walked over to the fountain and began to gulp down water.

Inside the library, the cool air welcomed them with a hug. Abby checked out her usual mystery books and Sam went to the nonfiction section. He got some books on bugs and another on inventions. What Abby called his 'geeky' books.

Sam looked at the clock on the library wall. "I guess we better get back," he said, hoping Abby wanted to stay.

Abby packed her books up. "That paper won't tape itself," she said and gave Sam a smile.

Back on their bikes, they coasted down Hill Street, turned left onto Jackson, and parked their bikes outside the barn.

Sam was relieved Joey Gordon had not appeared.

"The odd-meter says five miles," Abby announced.

Ignoring the odd-meter comment, Sam asked, "What's four plus one plus five? Come on, Abby, we're clocking your miles for the fitness badge!"

Hesitating, Abby said, "Ten, of course."

# CHAPTER SEVEN

Sam wrote 'library, the date, and five miles' into his notebook. He closed it up and shook his head sadly. "Only twenty-five more miles to go," he muttered.

Abby replied, "Easy-peasy."

Maybe for you, Sam thought, as he calculated how many more days he'd have to ride his bike to earn that fitness badge. He was relieved when he heard his Mom call them for lunch.

Arriving at the kitchen table, Sam was glad to see his Mom had made him a BLT sandwich and a pile of potato chips. "How do you live on that stuff?" he asked Abby, who was eating a salad with fresh vegetables and bits of apple in it.

Abby smiled. "I have to stay fit for soccer. You should try it sometime. All that greasy food makes you…"

"Fat?" Sam said, angry that his sister thought he was fat.

Abby smiled. "No, not fat. But if you ate a little healthier, you'd feel a lot better."

Sam said, "Mind your own business."

Abby bit her lip and finished her lunch.

Sam ate his sandwich and had a donut for desert. "I'm ready," he said, and got up from the table.

Abby looked at her mother. "If we had some music, it might make the job go faster."

Mom let them use her Ipad to listen to music while they worked in the barn.

Sam was still angry Abby made fun of what he ate, so he worked silently at the far end of the barn.

Abby wished she could say something to make Sam understand that she wasn't making fun of him, just trying to help. Sometimes, her twin could be so stubborn. Not like me at all, she thought.

They taped five hundred more pieces of paper.

Abby thought the music was helping. Working a little slower and taking a few short breaks seemed to help, too.

Sam found the work was calming him down. He was no longer angry at

Abby.

About three o'clock, Abby felt someone was watching them from the door. She was surprised to see Owen Parker peering at them. She pretended not to see him, but wondered how long he'd been there. Was he spying for Joey?

Sam saw Abby casting glances at the door and suddenly saw Owen. What the heck was he doing here? He searched to see if Joey was sneaking around with Owen, his best bud, his stooge. "What do you want here, Owen?" he asked, standing up.

"What are you doing?" Owen asked.

Abby smiled. "We're working on a top-secret experiment."

Sam glared at Owen, wishing Abby would shut up.

"What kind of top-secret experiment?" Owen asked, "It just looks like you're taping a lot of paper together."

Abby said, "We've got to tape this paper together to do the experiment."

Owen aimed his eyes again at all the paper.

Abby continued, "See this pencil? Well, Sam learned that this pencil can last 35 miles!"

"No way!" Owen said. "No pencil can last that long."

"Well, that's what my brilliant mad scientist brother is trying to find out," Abby said. Owen looked thoughtfully at the paper and then said, "Can I help?"

Sam said, "No, thanks."

Abby shot him a surprised look.

Owen sighed. "Well, good luck. See, ya, Abby." Then he aimed his eyes at Sam. "I only wanted to help." He turned and walked out of the barn.

Abby whirled on her brother, "Why didn't you let Owen help us?"

Sam saw she was angry. To distract her, he asked, "What's one thousand times two?"

"Five thousand," Abby shot back at him . "No, it's two thousand." She walked over to him. "Why didn't you let Owen help? An extra set of hands would be great."

Sam saw she was not letting it go. "Okay, I don't trust Joey, so I'm not sure about Owen, either."

"All he wanted was to help us," Abby said.

## CHAPTER SEVEN

"It could be a set-up, with Gordon sending Owen over here to spy on us."

"You're paranoid," Abby said. "I learned that in a movie." She laughed.

Sam shook his head. " Anyway, how about tomorrow, we take a break like Dad said? What if we bike to Pinky's for burgers and fries?" He saw Abby still was angry. " I'll use my allowance."

"As long as you're treating," Abby said, still angry he'd pushed Owen aside.

Sam stared at his sister as she went back to work on the paper pile. He wondered if she'd ever understand why he couldn't trust Owen or anyone friendly with Joey Gordon.

# Chapter Eight

Day five of summer vacation was cloudy and cool. Abby suggested that they ride to Pinky's as part of their biking project.

"It's going to rain," Sam said.

"That means it will be a little cooler," Abby replied.

Between bites of blueberry pancakes, Sam nodded.

The rain held off 'til they turned left on Main Street and parked behind the restaurant.

Sam munched on a juicy hamburger and fries.

Abby ate her burger but left the roll and half her fries.

"See, I told you it was going to rain," Sam said staring out the window. Abby gazed out the window and said, "The clouds dumped enough water to fill the town swimming pool!"

Sam felt relieved he'd have more time to rest up before the bike ride back. "Let's wait this one out."

Abby played with her fork, eager to get back to work on their project. "Hey, Sam, the rain stopped."

Sam groaned. He had been about to order an ice cream sundae. "How can you eat a burger without a roll? That's weird!"

Abby laughed.

Wiping their bikes off, the twins headed home.

Sam was surprised that his legs weren't achy. Maybe it's because the rain cooled things off, he thought.

As usual, Abby burst his good thoughts with, "The odd-meter says four miles."

## CHAPTER EIGHT

Rolling his eyes, Sam asked, "What's ten plus four?"

"It's fourteen! You see, I'm getting better at math and you're riding your bike better."

Sam wondered if it was true. "Let's go tell Mom we're back," he said.

Walking into their mother's art studio, they saw she was busy. painting.

Abby said, "Guess what, Ma! We've biked fourteen miles so far."

"And taped together two thousand sheets of paper," Sam added.

Mom looked up. "That's wonderful, kids." She looked at Sam. "You rode fourteen miles too?"

Sam nodded, a little surprised still that they'd already gone that far.

Mom smiled. "I think you deserve a reward. How would you like to go bowling?"

Sam shook his head. "No can do. We have work to do."

"Can we go bowling? *Pleeeaase.* We'll get back to work tomorrow," Abby promised.

Mom looked at Sam. "If you weed the flower beds by the front porch, I'll pay you in advance so you can go bowling today."

"Great!" Abby and Sam said at the same time and looked at each other. They both said the exact same word.

Mom laughed. "This project is good for you. You're even beginning to sound alike."

Abby and Sam looked at each other again.

The cool drizzly air wrapped around them as they biked to the bowling alley.

Abby thought that Sam was going a bit faster up Hill Street this time. She didn't have to double back as much.

After a quick left onto Broad Street, Sam saw the big blue and yellow Bowlorama sign. He realized he'd hardly worked up a sweat.

Abby was already through the door.

Because of the rain, tons of kids were in the bowling alley.

Sam and Abby walked toward the lane when Sam spotted Joey Gordon about to throw a ball.

Joey's buddy, Owen, turned just as Sam was trying to walk by without being noticed. Owen waved.

Sam scowled.

Abby waved back.

Sam gave Owen a small wave and hurried to the lane.

"Owen's nice," Abby said.

"Let's play," Sam said.

Sam and Abby bowled two games. She was the gutter ball queen and Sam was the king of splits. He was knocking pins down like he'd never done before.

Abby smiled. "I never knew you could bowl that good."

Sam smiled back. "I didn't either. Let's grab a snack and head for home."

Abby and Sam headed to the snack bar.

Abby saw her friend, Emma Smith and waved.

Emma waved back. "Hi Abby. Hi Sam."

Abby glanced at Sam. Was he blushing? She laughed and sat down next to Emma.

Sam looked uncomfortable, but joined them.

Emma smiled. "So, what are you two up to this summer?"

That was like pulling the cork out of a bottle. Abby jumped in and started telling Emma all about their project.

Emma seemed interested and kept glancing at Sam until Abby asked her to help paper tape. She looked at her hands and said, "I'd love to help, but I'm way too busy."

Suddenly she's too busy, Abby thought. *Who wants to tape thousands of pieces of paper together? It's as much fun as reading one of Sam's geeky books.* "Okay, well, we have to go. Come on, Sam. We have important work to do."

"Maybe, I'll see you later," Emma said to Sam.

Sam stood. "Abby and I have important work to do." He followed Abby out of the bowling alley, still not believing he'd turned Emma down. "I didn't even grab a soda," he exclaimed to Abby.

"No, you didn't," Abby said, "Not bad, Bro."

"Not bad at all," Sam agreed and hopped on his bike. "Beat ya to the barn," he shouted and stomped down on his pedal.

# CHAPTER EIGHT

Back at the barn, Abby announced, "The odd-meter says six miles. Wow!"

Sam smiled, "What's fourteen plus six?"

Abby said, "Twenty!"

"That's right," Sam said, noticing his sister was getting faster with her math problem solving. He logged the miles in his notebook.

The rest of day five, Sam and Abby worked on taping more pages of paper together.

"Dinner time!" Mom called.

Sam jumped up. "I could have gone longer," he said to Abby.

Abby was busy counting. "Sam, we did three thousand sheets of paper!"

"That can't be right," Sam thought, counting the packs of paper still on the shelf, believing Abby's poor math skills had struck again. "You're right," he exclaimed. "We're doing it!"

At dinner, Dad said, "Looks like you two are on a roll!"

Sam smiled at Abby and said, "No more rolls for me right now. With Abby's help, I'm working on getting that fitness badge as well as my science badge."

Abby and Sam were tired from their long day. But then Mom said, "Abby, Sam, you have about an hour before it gets dark to weed the flower beds like you promised."

This time, Abby groaned.

Sam said, "Come on, Abby, we can do it."

They pulled weeds, swept them up and put them into a bag. They finished just as the sun set.

Abby said, "I'm pooped."

"Tomorrow is Sunday," Sam said.

Abby laughed. "A day off? Fantastic!"

Sam shook his head. "After lunch at Grandma's, we gotta do more paper taping or we'll fall behind."

Abby made a wry face.

"No excuses," Sam said and was surprised Abby said it at the same time. They both looked at each other. How long could this togetherness last?

# Chapter Nine

Monday was day six of summer vacation.

Abby stared at Sam. He wasn't gorging on French toast. "Do you feel okay?" she asked. "You're not eating your breakfast."

Sam poked at his French toast with a fork. "Usually French toast cheers me up, but not today. Guess I'm tired."

Putting her head down on the table, Abby muttered, "If I tape one more piece of paper today, I'll scream."

Sam smiled. "Hey, Sis, I can't finish this project myself. We're doing fine, but we have to keep on working or we'll never get it done."

"Chill out, Sam. It's just the end of our first week of summer vacation. Can't we just bike today and paper tape tomorrow? Please?" Abby fixed her eyes on her brother.

Sam shook his head. "Sure, you're gonna get your fitness badge by biking around town."

"Well, you'll get one, too," Abby replied.

"Maybe. But I won't get my science badge, the one I really want, 'til we prove the pencil part. I've got a lot at stake here."

Abby whispered, "I promise this will be the last time we put off the paper taping. Please?"

Sam took a deep breath, "OK. Just don't keep doing this. I really want to see if the pencil experiment works. Don't you?"

Abby nodded.

Sam spread out a map of Jackson City.

Their mom walked by. "Are you two biking near the Superama? I need some cereal, milk and bananas."

Abby and Sam both said, "Sure" at exactly the same time and looked at each other in amazement.

Mom laughed. "I swear you two are becoming more twinnish every day. Here's a list and some cash."

"This is a lot," Sam said.

Mom shrugged. " I need to finish Mr. George's portrait. It's a surprise present from Mrs. George. His birthday is in two days."

Sam knew his mother always got nervous when she had a deadline for her paintings. "Okay, Ma," he said. "Abby, let's go."

They picked up their bikes at the garage and headed down the street.

Guess Who stood on his front porch as the twins rode by. "If it isn't the Jackson duo!" Joey snickered.

Sam pedaled faster. Abby heard Joey's laughter untl she turned up Hill Street. It made her angry, but there wasn't anything she could do about it if Sam didn't want to do something about it now.

This time, she saw Sam made it up the hill without much huffing or puffing.

*Too bad Joey didn't see that*, she thought .

Sam was thinking the same thing.

Superama was next to Pinky's. Sam and Abby ate their snack outside at a picnic table. Abby stared at a spider weaving its web while Sam waved to the Baker sisters as they whizzed by on new bicycles. He daydreamed about getting a brand new bright blue bike with flames painted on the sides. *That will have to wait until October unless I hit a growth spurt*, he thought.

"Abby calling. Is Sam Jackson here?"

That snapped Sam out of his trance. "Let's go," he said, eager to get back to work on his science project.

Walking up and down the Superama aisles, the twins got everything on Mom's list. After paying for everything, they separated the items into their backpacks.

"I don't want to take that big box of cereal. Your backpack is bigger than mine," said Abby.

"I don't have much room. I put the milk carton and bananas in my backpack so they don't get crushed.."

Abby pushed the cereal box into her pack.

"You crushed it," Sam said. "Mom won't be happy about that."

Abby took off on her bike with Sam right behind her. Suddenly, the cereal box flew out of her pack and Sam ran right over it. "Look what you did," Abby shouted. "You crushed the cereal box."

Sam picked up the box. "Mom won't be happy about this." He burst into laughter.

"What's so funny?" Abby asked.

Sam said, "Now it will fit your pack with no trouble. He shoved the box back into Abby's pack. And they both started to laugh.

Finally the twins were able to bike home. They coasted downhill most of the way and didn't look at each other so they wouldn't start giggling again.

Parking by the barn, Abby, still thinking about how Sam rode over the cereal box, announced, "The odd-meter says four miles."

Sam didn't ask her to add this time. He just wrote twenty-four in the notebook.

Abby picked up the cereal box. "Here we go," she said as they headed for the house.

In the kitchen Mom was excited., "Guess what? I finished the painting. Come see!"

Sam rushed over.

When Mom wasn't looking, Abby snuck the lopsided box of cereal into the cabinet and then hurried to the studio.

In Mom's studio, Sam saw Mr. George's portrait on the easel. He was surprised to see that Mr. George was wearing his Navy uniform and was smiling proudly. "He looks good," Sam said.

"Mrs. George gave me this old photo to use," said Mom.

"He's got hair!" shouted Abby, bursting into the studio.

"And he's much thinner," Sam said. Lately Sam had noticed he looked a bit thinner, too.

Mom sighed. "I hope Mr. George likes it."

Sam smiled. "I know he will. Right Abby?"

## CHAPTER NINE

Abby nodded.

Mom smiled back. "Let's go eat lunch. I made tuna sandwiches with raisins, your favorite, Abby." She looked at Sam. "Pizza, honey?"

Sam looked at the portrait again and replied. "Tuna, but no raisins, and on Abby's whole wheat bread will be great."

Mom and Abby almost fell over.

Sam didn't notice the surprise on their faces. He was thinking of another afternoon in the barn taping all those sheets of paper together and wondering if all this effort would really work.

# Chapter Ten

"Nothing like a tuna and raisin sandwich," said Abby.

Sam smiled.."Now we have energy to get back to paper taping, right, Abby?"

"Don't hate me, Sam, but I'd rather go to the pool this afternoon.'

Sam shook his head. "Abby, you promised. Now you're going back on your word. "

"Sam, I'm tired and hot. Let's take a break, like Dad says. It will help us work better afterwards."

Sam sighed.

"Tell ya what, Sam. Let's see who gets changed into our swimsuits first. Last one back here has to tape an extra one hundred sheets of paper. Okay?"

"Game on!" Sam said and sprang up the steps like a cheetah. He quickly changed into his swim trunks, put on his sandals and grabbed a towel. But when he got to the bottom of the stairs, Abby was waiting for him.

"Beat ya," Abby said, a sly smile on her face.

Looking down, Sam mumbled, "You tricked me. But you better keep your promise this time."

Abby called to her Mother in the studio, "Mom, we're biking to the pool."

In a way, Sam was glad Abby won. A dip in the town pool would refresh them so they could work on their project better.

Once on their bikes, they turned right onto Hill Street, then left on Main. As always, Sam was relieved Joey was nowhere to be seen.

After parking their bikes on the rack in front of the pool, they found a spot for their beach towels next to their friends Luke, Emma and Brady.

# CHAPTER TEN

Abby was chatting away while Sam was worried about taking off his shirt in front of the other kids. He'd almost forgot how self-conscious he was about his weight.

Abby saw Emma looking at Sam. "Let's go in the water," she said.

Sam hesitated and then removed his shirt. Emma was still smiling at him. He felt fine. In fact, he had to tie his bathing suit tighter. I'm really losing weight, he thought as he followed the others into the pool.

The cool water soothed their sore muscles. Abby was still talking to her friends when a shadow passed overhead.

"It looks like rain," Emma said to Sam.

Sam smiled awkwardly. What could he say to her? "We have to go anyway. We have a lot of work to do."

"On your project?" Emma asked. "Abby told me about it."

Sam nodded. "Want to help? We can use help."

A voice above them sounded familiar. "Yeah, Lardo, you can use a lot of help!"

Sam looked up.

Joey Gordon's eyes were blasting him from above.

Sam looked back for Emma, but she was gone. Maybe she hadn't heard what Joey said.

Abby was glaring at Joey.

Sam knew his twin had heard Joey's nasty remarks. He turned to Joey and was about to tell him to jump in a lake, but there was a loud crash of thunder and dark clouds rolled in.

Joey was running for the gate.

Abby shouted, "Sam, come on. We have to get home."

Sam wished he'd had time to answer Joey, but he knew staying in the water with thunder and lightning was too dangerous. Still fuming, and wondering if he could find the courage to fight Joey, he ran for his bike.

Sam and Abby got home minutes before the rain came.

After parking his bike, Sam headed for the stacks of paper without saying a word to Abby.

Abby saw Sam was still upset. "The odd-meter says four miles." She smiled at Sam as she said it, hoping it would make him feel better.

Sam gave her a small smile. He understood what she was doing. "What's twenty-four plus four?" he asked.

In a flash, Abby said, "Twenty-eight."

Sam nodded. "Abby, we only have seven more miles to bike our thirty-five miles and earn our Fitness badges."

Abby nodded happily.

Sam frowned. "But we still have two thousand sheets of paper left to tape."

Abby stared at the packages of paper and with her teasing smile said,"Yeah, but, you have an extra one hundred, Sam. Remember?"

"How could I forget that!" Sam replied. "You're pretty sneaky, twin sister," he teased.

Abby laughed.

The next day, Mom asked them to clean their rooms again, so they didn't get to the barn until almost ten-thirty in the morning.

Abby counted out one hundred pieces of paper and handed them to Sam.

Sam took the papers and said, "That's the last time you trick me." Then he laughed.

The morning went quickly and they were still working when Mom called them for lunch.

Sam ate what Abby ate and downed it with a cold glass of water. "I'm ready to go," he said and charged toward the barn.

Abby was beginning to wonder if having an energetic brother was such a great idea after all.

The afternoon in the barn dragged on with just the music as their only distraction. From time to time, they got up, stretched, and drank water, but they kept on going.

Sam said, "I wish we could use that fan in the corner over there, but it will mess up our paper roll. We'll have to settle for sweating, I guess."

Around four-thirty, Abby finished her pile of paper and let out a loud yawn. "I'm done. I'm gonna take a shower. See you at dinner."

"See ya later," Sam said, still bent over, working.

When Mom called for dinner, Sam still wasn't in the house.

## CHAPTER TEN

"He's usually the first one at the table. I'll see if he's in the barn," Abby said.

There was Sam, sleeping, stretched out with their cat, Whiskers, tucked in against his chest.

Abby laughed. He had a fistful of untaped pages in his right hand.

Abby ran back to the house to grab a camera. This was what their mother called a photo-op. She aimed the camera and fired.

The flash lit up the barn.

Sam woke up. "What was that? How long have I been sleeping?"

Abby said, "I left the barn at four-thirty. It's past six o'clock now." She looked at the paper in Sam's hand. "Did you finish?"

Looking around, still half-asleep, Sam yawned and then replied, "Almost."

Feeling sorry for him, Abby stayed and helped Sam tape the rest of the sheets..

Then they added their new pieces to the huge, uneven, roll of paper.

"Thanks, Abby. That almost makes up for your tricking me." Sam forced a smile.

Sam closed the barn and they headed for the house.

At dinner, Sam announced, "We've almost got one mile of paper done."

Abby added, "We only have one thousand pages left to tape."

Sam chuckled. Now, she gets good at math.

Their mother smiled. "Then you'll see if a pencil can really write a line thirty-five miles long."

"I still don't believe it," Abby said, "But my mad scientist brother and I are going to prove it one way or another. Right Bro?"

Sam could only yawn.

That night Sam dreamt that he and Abby were riding on a giant pencil in the sky. As it wrote across the blue, it got smaller and smaller. When it got really tiny, they tried to hold on, but slipped off and fell toward the earth. They were screaming and flapping their arms as Sam saw he was about to smash into their own barn.

When Sam awoke, he remembered his dream and wondered if it was trying to warn him that this crazy experiment was doomed.

# Chapter Eleven

On day nine of summer vacation, Mom hugged Sam as she did most mornings. "Hey, you look different. Taller and older."

"Thanks!" Sam smiled. "I'll probably never be skinny like Abby. Dad says I'm built like a fire plug, like him. But I think I've lost some weight with all the biking and paper taping."

At breakfast, Dad loaded up his waffles with butter and syrup.

Sam looked at Abby's waffle which was covered only with fresh fruit. He skipped the butter and just used a little maple syrup on his waffles with some fresh blueberries.

Between bites, Abby asked, "What're we doing today?"

Sam looked thoughtful and said, "How about we finish the paper taping and then ride to the Ice Cream Shack after lunch to celebrate?"

"My treat," Mom said. "You two have worked really hard and Dad and I are proud of you."

Sam and Abby raced happily to the barn. But when they got to there, they were in for a big surprise. Their lumpy-bumpy lopsided roll of paper was scattered in pieces across the barn floor. And the fan was blowing on high speed sending torn scraps everywhere

Sam stared in shock at the mess.

Abby turned to him and asked, "Did you turn on the fan?"

"Of course not! Did you?"

Abby shook her head. "I don't get it."

Sam frowned. "I do. This is sabotage. Someone is trying to wreck our project. And I think I know who did this. Don't you?"

They both said, "Joey Gordon."

Sam turned off the fan. "I know he did it, but without a witness, we can't prove it."

And coincidence of coincidences, guess who happened to show up? Owen Parker.

*Was he in on it, too?* Sam wondered.

Abby wondered the same thing, but the look on Owen's face when he saw the mess told her that he was as surprised as they were. "I was gonna ask how your project was going, but I see. How did this happen?"

Sam didn't want to answer him, still suspecting Owen knew something about what happened to the paper roll.

Abby sighed and said, "When we got here, papers were torn off the roll, the fan was on high speed and blowing scraps all over the barn."

Owen looked at the fan. "Did you guys leave it on maybe?"

Abby shook her head. "Neither of us turned on the fan—"

"But someone did," Sam added, glaring at Owen.

"Have you heard anything around town?" Abby asked, aiming her green eyes at Owen.

Sam approached Owen and said, "Tell the truth. Did you have anything to do with this?" his hands balled into fists.

Owen shook his head. "I would never do anything like this to you guys." He looked at Sam. "Maybe I can help fix it up for you? I'd like to help. What are you trying to do?"

Sam sighed and handed him the lemonade lid.

Owen read it aloud: "'The average lead pencil can draw a line thirty-five miles long.' So?"

"So we almost finished making a mile of paper so we can draw on it with the pencil. Now we gotta put it all back together," Abby said..

"So?" Owen said again..

Abby smiled. "We really could use help," she said.

Sam felt frustrated. "We have to see if the pencil can last drawing that long of a line. We'll earn science fitness badges. We've been biking around town and are almost done. Believe me, it wasn't easy biking thirty-five miles and taping up all this paper. Now we have to fix up this mess!"

"Wow, that's a lot of work. Good luck with that," Owen said, and he left as quickly as he came.

Sam said, "You see, I was right about him. Owen didn't really want to help us. Yes, it is a lot of work, and now it's even more work!" He looked at Abby. "Looks like it's just you and me."

Abby rubbed her chin. "I'd like to catch who did this."

Sam muttered, "So would I."

Abby smiled. "You know all those mystery books I read, that you tease me about? Well, I just got an idea from one of them. I think we should put a camera in the barn to catch the culprit."

"What a great idea!" Sam high-fived her. "Let's see if reading all those mystery novels pays off." He pounded his palm with his fist. "I can't wait to see if that Joey Gordon was behind this."

# Chapter Twelve

"How are we going to get this camera idea of yours to work?" Sam asked Abby.

Abby's mind raced through the plots of her favorite mystery books. "Maybe we can string a wire cable across the barn door inside to see if someone trips over it. Hmmm…we could check for fingerprints."

Sam sighed. "Fingerprint kits are expensive, and somehow we'd have to get ahold of Joey's fingerprints."

The more Abby thought about it, the more she thought that a security camera would do the trick. But how to get one was another problem. "Sam, I think we need to put a camera over the barn door."

Sam nodded, but said, "The problem is paying for it."

Abby sat down to think and suddenly smiled. "Remember Grandpa set up a camera over his woodshed when we were real little?"

Sam nodded. "He was so mad when someone stole his saw and chisel."

Abby nodded back. "I just finished reading 'The Secret of the Jelly Bean Thief.' They used a security camera. Turns out the thief was a squirrel."

Sam started laughing, picturing the camera catching the squirrel eating the jelly beans.

Abby was still thinking. "Sam, let's go ask Grandma if she still needs that camera."

Sam jumped to his feet. "Race ya."

Hopping on their bikes, they whizzed down the street to Grandma's house.

Abby was surprised at how much faster Sam was able to ride his bike. He actually beat her to Grandma's door.

"Well," Grandma said when she saw them, "what do I owe this visit to? Need more paper? I've got a bit left, but not much."

"No, Grandma," Sam said. "Someone went into our barn, turned the fan on high, and wrecked our roll of taped papers for the pencil experiment. We need a camera to catch him."

"Or her," Abby piped in. "Remember Grandpa's camera over the woodshed out back? Could we borrow it 'til we discover who done it?"

Grandma laughed. "Lordie, I forgot all about that camera your crazy old Grandpa installed. You're welcome to it. But it's high up and I'm not about to climb any ladders."

"I don't like bothering Dad," Sam said, "but he's tall. I'll ask him."

They biked back to their barn, picked up the loose papers, and worked all morning. The papers were rejoined into the lumpy-bumpy roll of paper, which was now more lumpy and bumpy than ever.

"We're back in business!" Abby said, wiping sweat off her forehead.

Sam unplugged the fan and carried it to the garage. "No one can do fan damage again. When Dad gets home, we'll ask if he can help us with the camera."

"Wanna ride to the Ice Cream Shack?"

Sam nodded and they headed out. First a left onto Jackson Street. Sam was almost hoping Joey would be there so he could find out if he had been the rat behind the sabotage. No such luck. Passing his yard, he turned right onto River Road and another right onto Back Street.

"Looks like a long line," Sam said when they reached the popular shop.

"Yeah, but their ice cream is so thick and creamy. It's worth waiting for," Abby said.

"You don't usually like ice cream," Sam said.

Abby laughed. "Of course, I do, but not when I'm in training."

Sam stared at the large poster of a Shack Special Sundae. "You've got great will power," he muttered.

"So do you. You're the one pushing us to finish this project. That's really great will power," Abby said.

"I didn't think about that before," Sam said, getting into line..

## CHAPTER TWELVE

Guess Who was behind them?

Sam and Abby looked at each other and wondered. *Another coincidence?*

# Chapter Thirteen

"Owen, what are you doing here?" Sam demanded.

"Sam, he's just having an ice cream, like us. Right Owen?" Abby smiled, glad she was between them.

Owen nodded.

Sam grunted.

Abby ordered her usual, a small root beer float.

Sam's mouth was watering for a Super Shack Sundae, but instead, he ordered a medium chocolate swirl ice cream cone. He kept turning his cone and licking fast.

Abby saw Owen watching and thought he was going to tease Sam about how he licked his cone. "Why do you spin your cone like that?" she asked Sam.

Sam smiled, "That's part of the fun."

Abby sighed, but saw Owen was walking toward them, a medium chocolate swirl ice cream cone in his hand. To her surprise, he was spinning it around and licking it too. "You and Sam eat your cones the same way," she exclaimed.

Owen looked at Sam and Sam looked at Owen. "I guess we do," Owen said.

"Why don't you sit with us?" Abby asked. "Sam, slide over. You two can slobber together."

Sam slid over.

Owen looked around the store and then slowly slid in next to Sam.

Abby watched as both boys spun their cones and licked up their ice cream. She wondered if maybe now they could be friends.

Owen spoke first. "I'm really sorry about what happened to you guys. You

## CHAPTER THIRTEEN

know the paper…"

"Thanks," Abby said.

Sam nodded.

"I really don't know—"

Abby interrupted. "I believe you."

Sam let out a deep sigh. "Okay." Maybe Owen wasn't such a bad kid. Maybe he deserved a chance. Dad says someone is innocent until proven guilty.

Owen stood up. "I have to go. Thanks for letting me sit with you."

Abby replied. "Come on over, sometime."

Owen nodded and left.

After they left the store, Sam and Abby hopped on their bikes.

Sam was surprised Owen was riding behind them. He was even more surprised when Owen drove past Joey's house and stopped his bike at their driveway. He was still suspicious, but decided to wait and see just what Owen was up to.

Abby announced, "That's three miles on the odd-meter."

"What's Abby talking about?" Owen asked as he entered the barn.

Sam pointed to the odometer on Abby's bike. "She means her odometer. It measures distance. We just rode three miles to the Ice Cream Shack and back." Turning toward Abby, Sam asked, "What's twenty-eight plus three?"

Owen blurted out, "Thirty-one."

"Way to go, Owen!" said Abby.

Owen laughed.

Sam smiled. Maybe Owen was okay after all. He showed Owen his notebook. "We already did 31 miles. Now we only have four miles left to bike before Abby gets her badge and I get my fitness badge, too."

Abby said, "We might get done with the paper taping soon too." She looked at Owen. "Wanna help?"

Sam hoped Owen had changed, that he might want to help them.

Owen glanced at his watch and said, "No. I'm sorry. I can't." He walked to his bike. See ya," he called back and pedaled away.

"I really thought he was going to help us," Abby said.

Sam snarled, "What do you expect? He's Joey's best friend. Maybe he's in on that bully's plot to stop us."

Abby shook her head. "I don't think so. I think he's okay."

Sam glanced at the camera. " Maybe. Anyway, we'll catch the rat who did this on the camera. Your friend, Owen, is either a good guy or a bad guy. But we'll soon find out."

"Sam, you're too suspicious. Maybe Owen just isn't into this project like we are. Dad always says that's why ice cream comes in lots of flavors. We're chocolate chip and Owen is vanilla. Who knows? We might convince Owen to like chocolate chip yet."

The twins sat on the front porch steps and waited for their father to come home.

"Well, lookie, lookie," their father said, "it's double trouble. What're you two up to?"

Abby told him about their intruder. "We asked Grandma if we could use Grandpa's camera over the woodshed. Remember it?"

"Oh, yeah." Dad scratched his head. "Grandpa was mighty angry. He never did catch the thief."

"Well, we want to catch the person who did this. But even on a ladder, I can't reach that high. Think you can help us?" Sam asked.

"With something like climbing a ladder, I'm glad you decided not to risk it yourselves," Dad said. "Safety first."

Sam and Abby both groaned and then looked at each other.

Dad drove them in his SUV down Jackson Street to Grandma's. They held the ladder as Dad climbed up and removed the camera. Next, he pulled and pulled until all the wires came out from the shed wall.. Then it was back to their barn to install the camera that would catch the rascal.

After dinner, Dad finished installing the camera over the barn door. He drilled a hole and ran the wires into the barn and Sam plugged them in. Then Sam plugged them into a DVR so it would send pictures to his laptop.

"Thanks Dad, Sam said, "You've been after us to clean out the garage. I promise I'll help with that after we finish the pencil pusher project. OK?"

"I'll help too," Abby said. "We're a team now. Right Sam?" She held up her fist.

## CHAPTER THIRTEEN

"It's a deal," Sam said and they fist-bumped.

Dad examined the camera. "By the way, kids, the camera only comes on if it detects movement, so you'll only get pictures sent to your computer if something is moving outside the barn."

" Thanks Dad," Sam said.

Abby did a few soccer kicks. "Watch out, Jackson City paper-wrecker. We're gonna catch you!"

Sam wondered if he'd ever be able to kick like that.

# Chapter Fourteen

The next morning, Sam was pale and didn't finish his breakfast.

Abby asked, "Are you sick?"

"I'm just feeling anxious since that setback with the fan yesterday. This project is taking so much time and I don't know how it will turn out. So far, there's no photos from the barn camera. I can't believe we can't catch this rat."

"It seems like we've been biking and taping forever," said Abby. "But it's been less than two weeks so far. And anyway, you'll get your science badge whether the pencil makes the thirty-five mile line or not. Remember, Mr. Gordon said to show your work?"

"That makes me feel better, Abby. Thanks!" Sam said.

"I'll go check on our paper roll while you finish breakfast," Abby offered.

Sam watched Abby leave. It really hadn't been so bad working with her after all.

Abby was back before Sam took his last spoonful of Fruiteos. "I guess the perpetrator stayed away last night too," she said, using her mystery book vocabulary. "Perpetrator. Culprit. Sabotage. Sleuth. Sam, not only are we scientists, but now we're sleuths. Don't worry, we'll solve this mystery or my name isn't Abby Jackson, Sam I am!"

Sam said, "I just got a link on my laptop showing you going into the barn. Guess the Sleuth Cam is working ."

Mom said, "Tell you what. When you two finish the mile of paper, I'll treat you to lunch at Vinnie's Pizza. How many miles do you have left to bike?"

"Four," they both said at once.

## CHAPTER FOURTEEN

Abby laughed. "Let's go, Bro. A paper-taping we must go."

They finished attaching the last two hundred and eighty sheets of paper. After a big high-five, they looked proudly at the roll in the middle of the barn. "This is a great moment in the Jackson twins lives," Sam said.

"We need a pic of this." Abby ran to get Mom for the photo op.

The twins stood behind the giant roll, smiled and said, "Paper!" while their mother took their picture.

Then Mom gave them a twenty-dollar bill and off they biked to Vinnie's.

Sam was feeling great as he turned left onto Jackson.

You Know Who was standing in the middle of the street. "Hey Lardo, where are you off to in such a hurry?" He spied Abby coming down the road. "With your sister again, huh? Well, I guess I better let you pass or your sister might beat me up." He let out an evil laugh and walked to the side of the road.

Sam spotted Owen behind the Gordon's fence. I knew he was a rat, he told himself as he pedaled faster down the road. Still angry, Sam made a left onto River Road, another left onto Main, and parked in the side parking lot.

Abby caught up and saw Sam looked upset. "Are you all right?" she asked, not knowing about his incident with Joey and Owen.

"I'm fine," Sam said and held the door open for her.

Abby nearly flew into her seat. "Sipping on root beers and munching on a veggie pizza is a great treat for finishing our paper taping," she said.

Sam was deep in thought. 'Wanna start writing our lines when we get home?" he asked, not wanting to hear Abby advise him about what to do about Joey and Owen.

"Absotively!" Abby clapped her hands. "Can't wait!"

They ate quickly and then hopped back on their bikes. Sam was relieved Joey wasn't around as he pedaled past the Gordon's house.

Reaching their barn, Abby checked the odometer. Putting her hands up to her mouth as if playing a bugle, she said, "Doo, doo, doo! Hear ye, hear ye, hear ye. The odometer says four miles!"

"You said 'odometer!'" Sam said.

"Yeah, I was just yanking your chain, Sam," Abby said. "That's what sisters do."

"I figured as much. You're an odd one yourself, Abby Jackson!"

Sam logged in the last four miles, the date, and wrote thirty-five. He circled it. When they went inside, they gave Mom their change from Vinnie's and Sam showed her the notebook.

"Wow! You two did it! I'm proud of you both," their mother said.

Sam said, "Ma, we need a new pencil."

Ma smiled, "Help yourself. That's the least I can do to help my two mad scientists."

Grabbing a pencil from the kitchen drawer, Sam quickly sharpened it and then handed the sharpener to Abby. "Hey partner, I'll draw and you can sharpen. But not too much!"

Abby smiled, put the little sharpener in her pocket, and they headed to the barn.

Just as they were making a plan of action, a shadow caught Sam's eye.

Owen stuck his head in. "What's up, guys?"

Sam was silent.

Abby smiled. "This is a momentous occasion, Owen. Sam and I are about to begin writing the thirty-five miles of lines with this brand-new pencil."

Sam said, "Abby, he's not interested in helping us."

Owen said, "Writing that much with a pencil is a lot of work. Let me see your pencil?"

Sam held it up like a trophy.

Owen frowned. "And you really think that pencil can last for 35 miles?"

Abby said, "That's what we want to find out. Wanna help?"

Owen's brow wrinkled. "We just got new carpet in the hallway. I watched the workers unroll it, cut it, and nail it down. What if Abby holds one end and I unroll the paper while you do the writing? She can roll up her end as we go along. Would that work?"

"Super idea, Owen," Abby said.

Sam stared at Owen. "Did you just say you'd help us? Yesterday, you said it was too much work."

Abby crossed her fingers behind her back. She was no math whiz like Sam, but she realized this would go much faster with three people.

## CHAPTER FOURTEEN

"Well.," Owen stammered and shifted his feet from side to side. "It's just that my parents got divorced last year. Mom works a lot more now and sometimes she needs me to stay with Grandma."

"You take care of your Grandma?" Sam said, surprised that Owen had a caring side.

Owen nodded. "When Grandma feels well, a bus picks her up and takes her to the Senior Center. If she's having a bad day, with her arthritis, she has trouble walking. Then she stays home and needs my help."

Abby smiled. "I think that's great," she said.

Sam nodded, thinking he'd misjudged Owen. "If you want to help—"

Owen sighed. "I really want to help you both, but I might not be able to come every day."

Sam said, "Thanks, Owen. I understand. Come when you can."

Abby said, "We're wasting time! Let's roll."

"Unroll," Owen laughed.

Sam watched as Abby and Owen walked over to the large roll of paper. He'd thought he was going to do this project all on his own, but realized now that he was glad it had turned into a team project. He wondered if Owen was really going to be part of the team.

Abby and Owen unrolled the ball of paper as far as it would go in the barn.

Sam bent down and began to draw a line down the paper as Abby unrolled it on one end and Owen rolled up on the other end.

"This is tough work," Sam said after a while.

"We can do it," Abby said, but her back was aching, too.

Sometimes the pencil poked through the paper and Sam would get angry.

"I'll be right back," Abby said after this happened several times..

Sam looked at Owen. "Thanks for helping out," he said.

Owen nodded.

Abby soon returned and slid a large flat piece of cardboard under the paper. It was left over from a refrigerator box.

"Great idea, Abby," Owen said, giving her a smile.

Sam thought he saw Abby blush.

It took the rest of the afternoon to unroll, draw the line, and reroll the paper.

Abby only sharpened the pencil once.

Sweat poured off them. .

"Anyone want a popsicle?" Sam asked, taking a stretch.

They sat on the front porch steps. As they licked their popsicles, their lips changed colors. Sam's were red, Owen's blue and Abby's green like her eyes.

"What are you doing with them?" A harsh voice interrupted their break.

"What's up, Gordo?" Owen asked, looking uneasy.

Joey stared at Sam. "Not much." He turned to Owen. "Wanna play miniature golf tomorrow, Owen?"

Sam had a feeling Owen was going to desert them for Joey.

Abby looked like she was gearing up for a soccer kick..

Owen shook his head. "Not tomorrow, man. I'm helping Sam and Abby with their big project. Maybe I can catch ya later, after we're finished."

Sam was stunned. He saw Joey glaring but ignored him.

Joey looked like he wanted to say something to Owen but got on his bike.

Owen said, "S'long, Joey."

Joey looked back and then rode away.

Abby was grinning like the cat that just ate the canary.

Sam still didn't believe Owen could have changed this much but sat and finished his ice pop.

When Owen finished his pop, he stood up and walked to his bike. "See you guys tomorrow," he said.

As Owen rode off, Abby said, "Looks like Owen is turning into a chocolate chip kinda guy after all."

Sam replied, "I sure hope he sticks with us. It will make our project go much faster."

Abby laughed. "If he does, I'll bake him a whole batch of chocolate chip cookies!"

*If he does?* Sam wondered if Owen was really ready to risk his friendship with Joey, the bully to work with them. He still suspected Owen was a rat.

## Chapter Fifteen

The next morning, Sam and Abby hurried to his computer. "Maybe we caught the rat on camera last night," Abby said.

Sam turned on his computer. "So far, no action on the Sleuth Cam. Wait a minute!" He stared hard at the screen. A photo flashed on his monitor. "It's a squirrel," Sam said.

"Can squirrels turn on fans?" Abby asked.

Sam laughed. "Who knows? We'll have to watch out for this nut. Let's get to work."

Owen showed up around ten o'clock just as they were unrolling the humungous paper roll. He gave them a hello and walked right to his post at the end of the roll.

Sam smiled. Owen seemed to be joining the team after all.

Abby and Owen worked the roll of paper while Sam drew the line with his pencil. It was hard work on all three of them, so they were glad when Mom called them for lunch.

Owen stayed for lunch, too.

Abby asked Owen about his grandmother and Owen told her how he enjoyed reading books and watching soap operas with his Granny.

Sam was mostly silent but was beginning to admire how Owen cared for his family. He was surprised when his mother whispered, "I like your new friend, Sam." He almost said Owen isn't my friend, but stopped himself.

"This is hard work," Owen said, stretching his arms to the sky.

When the second mile-long line was drawn, Sam tallied it into his notebook. Abby said, "Two down and thirty-three to go."

Owen laughed. "Only thirty-three to go? See you tomorrow." He waved and hopped onto his bike.

"I'm gonna put the notebook and pencil in a safe place. Be back in a sec," Sam said. He put The Pencil in his blue pencil box and placed it in his top right desk drawer with The Notebook. This was super-valuable property. He used his key to lock the drawer. Then he placed the key under the hamster cage in his room. "Germie, you guard this key with your life," he said and laughed at his pet racing around on the wheel in the center of the cage.

The next morning, Abby ran to the barn.

Sam wasn't surprised that Owen didn't show up.

"Maybe he has to take care of his grandma," Abby said.

Sam had a feeling Owen had enough of helping them with their insane project. "It doesn't matter. Let's get started."

Things went a lot slower without Owen. Hearing thunder, Abby got nervous. The loud noise and lightning scared her ever since she was a little girl. "We better stop," she said.

"We have to keep going," Sam urged, "We're on a roll."

Soon the rain hit the metal barn roof.

"It's so loud," Abby said.. "But what's that other sound?"

Drip, drip, plop. Drip, drip, plop.

"Oh, no!" Sam grabbed an old plastic bucket and placed it under where the barn ceiling was leaking.

"First the fan. Now our enemy is water!" Abby shouted over the heavy rain. "All our paper will be ruined."

Sam shook his head and ran out of the barn.

Abby wondered where he was going?

When he returned, he was soaking wet, but had a big bundle in his arms. "Help me with this," he said.

Abby got up and together they pulled a large black tarp from the bundle. "Great idea," Abby said, amazed Sam had carried this heavy tarp by himself in the rain.

They put the tarp on top of the paper roll to protect it.

Sam shook water off himself and said, "When the rain stops, I think we

## CHAPTER FIFTEEN

should move the paper roll to the garage. I've never seen a leak there."

Abby sighed. "I guess we'll have to move it back and forth to the barn every day. We need a big space to unroll our paper, right?"

"It's too big and heavy," Sam said. Looking around the barn, he spotted an old wheelbarrow. "It's full of dust from Dad's rock garden project. We can clean it up when the rain stops."

Waiting for the rain to stop, Sam and Abby walked around the barn, checking for more leaks.

Abby said, "Looks like that's the only leak, but we still have to be careful. We're so close to finishing. I really don't want to risk having our paper ruined."

Sam nodded. "It was quite a job, wasn't it?"

Abby stared at the huge roll of paper. "Ya know, Sam, I was thinking."

"Uh, oh," Sam said. "You thinking is scary." He laughed. "I'm joking. You do get some good ideas, once-in-a-while.".

Abby tossed him a scowl and said,"Since we're done with the biking part, why don't we draw two lines a day, so we can finish in half the time?"

"Why didn't I think of that?" Sam said. "You have a good point. Maybe there's a better way to do this."

They both said, at the same time, "Let's sleep on it," And burst into laughter.

When the the rain finally stopped, they got some old brushes and a broom and scrubbed away the dirt from the wheelbarrow. Next Sam hosed it down.

Abby said, "I'm hungry. Let's get a snack while this wheelbarrow dries out."

Sam wondered why he didn't feel hungry. Usually, after an hour of watching T.V. or sitting at the computer, he was famished. Could working so hard keep him from wanting snacks? He followed Abby to the kitchen.

"Want a soda?" Abby asked, cutting up an apple and some cheese.

Sam said, "I'll have what you're eating."

So it was cheese and apple slices on the front porch. They sat there quietly, eating the sweet fruit but Sam was wondering if there was a faster way to finish the pencil experiment.

# Chapter Sixteen

After their snack, Sam and Abby went back to the barn to get back to the paper roll. They worked for several hours, but both were tired. "It's time to call it a day," Sam said.

"We still have to move the 'monster,'" Abby said, pointing to the huge roll of paper.

By now the wheelbarrow was dry .

Taking different sides of the roll, Abby said, "One, two, three, lift."

"Heave-ho," Sam said as they tried to lift the roly-poly, lumpy-bumpy ball of paper into the wheelbarrow. Abby lost her balance and Sam dropped his side on the ground.

"How much does this thingy weigh?" Abby said, giving the roll a disgusted look.

Sam sighed. "A lot. I don't know if this wheelbarrow can hold the weight." He scratched his head.

"We can't put the ball on a scale," Abby said.

Sam nodded. "Let's weigh the last package of paper."

Abby smiled. "Then we can multiply it by the number of packages we already used."

To get the total weight," Sam said. "You're becoming a math whiz," he said, giving his twin a big smile.

Abby dashed out saying, "I'll get Mom's bathroom scale."

When she returned, Sam placed the last ream of paper on the scale. "Looks like about five pounds."

Abby said, "So we used ten and a half packages."

# CHAPTER SIXTEEN

Sam nodded. "I figure this wacky paper ball weighs over fifty-two pounds!"

Abby said, "Wow. I weigh a bit over sixty-five pounds. No wonder we couldn't lift it."

Sam nodded.

Abby stared at the huge ball. " Just how're we gonna lift this monster? Can we cut it in half and make it into two smaller balls?"

Sam's face lit up. "I don't know if it's the mystery books you're reading, or if this project is making you smarter, but you sure come up with some great ideas!"

They unrolled the paper ball about halfway and removed the tape. Then Sam rolled up one ball and Abby the other.

"Now we have two smaller rolls instead of one monster," Abby said.

Sam smiled, "Each roll is half a mile and weighs about twenty-six pounds. It'll work. Great idea, Abby. We just have to make two trips to the garage instead of one."

"We can do this!" Abby said. .

Sam and Abby got on the opposite sides of the first roll. "Heave-ho!" They both said and lifted the roll onto the wheelbarrow.

"It worked," Sam said.

"Of course, it worked. It was my idea," Abby said with a chuckle.

"I'll wheel this one and you can wheel the next one," Sam offered, hoping the old wheelbarrow wouldn't collapse under the weight.

Abby followed behind Sam and the squeaking barrow. When they got to the garage, she said, "Hey, Sam, you just went from pencil pusher to wheelbarrow pusher."

After dumping the barrow, they rolled the first paper roll into an empty corner of the garage. "It will be safe here," Sam said.

They then went back to the barn and hefted the second roll onto the wheelbarrow. "Do you think you can push this?" Sam asked.

"Easy-peasy," Abby said.

Sam followed Abby to the garage and helped her unload the barrow. They left the wheelbarrow in the garage and locked the door.

"We better tell Mom and Dad so they don't accidentally get rid of our paper,"

Abby said.

"They might think they're paper monsters," Abby said and laughed.

After dinner, the twins sat outside on the porch swing.

Sam watched the lightning bugs flashing their lights off and on. "I wonder how they do that?" He asked aloud.

Abby laughed, "Hey, no more science projects…at least, not until we finish this one."

Sam laughed too, but said, "Are they sending us a signal?"

Abby looked at her brother. "You really are a mad scientist. But my brain just lit up with a new idea for our project."

Sam used to make fun of her ideas, but now leaned closer.

Abby said, "What if we drew two lines at a time instead of one?"

Sam sat back, thinking hard. "Brilliant! That might work!" Sam said. "Let's try it out tomorrow."

Abby got up from the bench. "All this thinking makes me tired. Good night, Sam."

Sam watched her leave then returned to staring at the fireflies. Someday, I'll find out how you work, he thought, and headed for his room. He was really beginning to feel like a mad scientist but wondered if they'd ever finish this first project.

# Chapter Seventeen

In the morning, the only photo from the Sleuth Cam was a raccoon walking in front of the barn door.

After a good breakfast of cereal, fresh fruit and milk, they were ready to start the day. They took turns wheeling the paper rolls back to the barn and were ready to unroll the first ball when Sam saw Owen standing by the door..

Abby walked toward Owen. "Hey, Owen, you missed the excitement yesterday. It rained really hard and we discovered a leak in the barn, so…"

Sam listened silently as Abby rattled on and on. He wondered why she bothered. Owen didn't care.

Abby was finishing up , "So we cut the roll in half and wheeled them to the garage." She patted the paper and said, "This is valuable property."

Sam was glad she finished. "We have work to do."

"You got that right," Owen said. "Let's roll." He walked over to the roll of paper.

"Oh, I forgot to tell you, we're gonna try to draw two lines at a time," Abby said.

"Good idea." Owen knelt down at his end of the first roll while Abby slid the cardboard under her end.

Taking the pencil out of his pocket, Sam drew one line and then another one parallel to it on the same sheet of paper. "Okay, don't roll it up until I finish drawing both lines," he said to Abby.

Abby nodded and shouted to Owen, "That was my idea." She pulled the first sheet toward her.

Sam laughed and said to Owen. "She gets good ideas…sometimes."

Owen kept unrolling the paper from his end. Sam drew two lines on each sheet and then Abby pulled the paper forward carefully and rerolled it.

"You know," said Owen, "it's much easier working with the two smaller rolls. Don't ya think?"

"Sure thing!" Sam and Abby said at the same time.. They gave each other that weird look like this can't be happening.

Sam was confused. We're finishing each other's sentences and saying the same things at the same time, he thought. He wondered if that happened with all twins. Another experiment?

"Sam, stop daydreaming," Abby shouted.

Sam got back to work.

They were like a factory. Abby had to stop them to sharpen the pencil twice. With the three of them working together, they quickly finished the first roll.

Owen said, "This didn't seem to take much longer doing the double line. Great idea, Abby!"

Abby smiled.

Sam said, "That's five down and thirty more to go." He rubbed his back as he got up from the barn floor. Being on his knees bent over the paper for hours wasn't an easy job. He had to admit Owen was a big help.

Abby asked, "Owen, would you do us the honor of wheeling the paper blobs back to the garage?"

Sam wondered how Owen would react.

Owen walked over to the barrow. "Sure, I would be honored. But, I've been thinking, since they're so valuable, let's give them a name. How about The Paper Mile?"

Abby said, "How about The Paper Thingies?"

Sam said, "What about "The Paper Scrolls?"

"Let's vote. You can only vote once," Abby said. "Hands up for The Paper Mile."

No hands went up.

"Hands up for The Paper Thingies." She raised her hand.

"Hands up for The Paper Scrolls." Sam raised his hand.

## CHAPTER SEVENTEEN

"Owen, you didn't vote," Abby said.

Owen looked sheepish. "I didn't think I could."

Sam looked at Owen and said, "You're part of the team, so you can vote."

Abby smiled. "Which one do you want?"

Owen smiled at Sam. "I like The Paper Scrolls."

Abby frowned. "Sam, you let him vote because you knew he was going to vote for you."

Sam shrugged.

"Doo, doo, doo!" Abby trumpeted. "Announcing that these paper thingies are now officially dubbed "The Paper Scrolls."

Sam walked over to Owen. "And you, Sir Owen, have the honor of wheeling The Paper Scrolls back to the garage."

Owen lifted the handles of the wheelbarrow and together they paraded to the garage, delivering The Paper Scrolls into their safe haven.

Since it was still daylight, they each got a bottle of lemonade and some oatmeal cookies, which they ate outside on the porch steps.

"These cookies are good," Owen said.

"Healthy too," Sam said.

Abby popped her lemonade lid and read, "Only female mosquitoes bite." She slapped her arm with her hand. , "I guess that was a girl mosquito!"

Owen said, "Watch out for those vicious females!"

Sam said, "I wonder how they can tell that?"

Abby nearly choked and said. "Hey, that's how this whole mess started. With these lemonade lids."

Owen popped his lid and read, "Dolphins sleep with one eye open." He looked at Sam. "Hmm, I didn't know that."

Abby laughed. "Sam, we are not going to check out how dolphins sleep."

Owen laughed. "That would be funny though." He closed one eye and pretended to snore.

Sam laughed and then read his lid, "If you shake a can of mixed nuts, the larger ones will rise to the top." He reread it and looked at Owen. "I don't know who goes around shaking cans of nuts or gets close enough to a sleeping dolphin to see if its eyes are closed or open. I'm having enough trouble proving that the average lead pencil can draw a line thirty-five miles long."

"Hey, we got this made in the shade," Owen said. He took a bite of his cookie and said, "I love your mom's cookies."

"Me, too," Abby and Sam said at the same time.

Owen shook his head. "You two keep saying the same things at the same time. That's amazing."

Sam and Abby looked at each other and smiled. "It is amazing," they both said.

Owen laughed. "You did it again."

Abby said, "When we finish our project, Owen, I'll bake a whole bunch of these cookies for you. Enough for you to even bring home for your mom and grandma."

Sam joked, "When we complete The Paper Scroll, it will rain down oatmeal cookies all over Jackson City. The Mayor might even declare the date, 'Oatmeal Cookie Day' to celebrate."

"We might have a cookie parade down Main Street," Owen said.

"Awesome!" Abby and Sam said.

"First we have to finish," Sam said. *Would that day actually happen?* he wondered.

# Chapter Eighteen

After a breakfast of Apple granola and fresh orange juice, Sam checked his computer for the Sleuth Cam snaps. Nothing but a few jumpy squirrels.

Abby wheeled The Paper Scrolls to the barn.

To their surprise, Owen Parker was waiting outside.

Sam said, "Great to see you, Owen."

Abby was grateful Owen helped her unload the paper scrolls.

"Get ready to unroll, Abby," Owen said. He drummed on his thighs as if he was making a drum roll. "Last night, I was thinking, wouldn't this pencil drawing go even faster if you drew five lines at a time, Sam? I know that seems like a lot, but we'd be cutting the unrolling and rerolling times."

Sam looked at the paper roll.

Abby said, "Sam, if you draw five lines on each sheet, that's four fewer times we have to unroll and reroll The Scrolls."

"Abby gave me the idea," Owen said.

Sam groaned. "I don't know if my knees can take it. I'll need a few breaks every once in a while. That will waste more time."

"I can draw the lines if you get tired," Abby said.

"Me too," Owen offered.

Abby headed for something she had spotted on a shelf. "And look over there. That's Mom's foam gardening pad that she kneels on when she's weeding."

Sam grinned, "You two are full of great ideas today. I should have thought of that earlier." He placed the pad under his knees. "Drawing five lines and using the foam gardening board under my knees! Let's get started!"

Owen raced over to his end of the barn. "Here we go," he shouted as he began to unroll the first ball of paper.

Abby leaned over her brother. "He really is helping us," she whispered.

Sam looked up, smiled, and then ducked down drawing five lines down the first sheet of paper. "Pull," he said and Abby gently pulled the first completed sheet toward her.

The new system was working great, but every so often, Abby had to stop the process to resharpen the pencil.

Sam was worried that the pencil was now half its original size.

When Mom called them for lunch, Sam said, "Perfect timing. I need a break."

Abby said, "Owen's idea is working."

Sam nodded and said, "Thanks, Owen. Staying for lunch?"

Owen smiled and said. "Thanks, Sam."

"You're welcome," Sam said and sat at the table on the porch. He wondered if Owen was really ready to become a friend. Abby seemed to have no doubt, chattering away with their new team mate, but he still was cautious. How could he trust someone who was a friend of Joey's?

The afternoon crawled by and finally Abby said, "Sam, you look bushed. Let me take over for a while."

Sam hated to give in, but was really exhausted.

So they switched places and finished the five lines on the second roll by four o'clock.

Abby surprised Sam by saying, "Twenty-seven minus five is twenty-two."

This summer project had definitely helped her learn her math facts.

It's helping me with my waistline too, Sam thought as he recorded five lines in his notebook."Thanks, you guys," he said, giving them a tired, but happy smile.

"If we keep this up," Owen said, "we'll finish in four and a half days. Way to go!" They fist-bumped and then all three heaved The Paper Scrolls, one by one, into the wheelbarrow and took them to the garage.

Sam offered Owen a popsicle from the extra freezer in the garage. He grabbed one for Abby as she wheeled in the last Paper Scroll. All three were

## CHAPTER EIGHTEEN

enjoying their ices on the front porch steps when Sam felt a chill.

You Know Who was staring at them from across the street.

Owen waved .

Joey stared at Owen.

Sam saw Joey had his little sister with him. Even a bully like Joey wouldn't do anything in front of his little sister. He watched as Joey walked away.

"Why didn't you wave to Joey?" Owen asked Sam.

Sam wondered if he could trust Owen. "It's a long story," he said. He didn't want Owen telling Joey.

Blabbermouth Abby blurted out, "It's cause Joey's been mean to Sam for years. He's a bully with a capital B. Bully!"

Sam cringed. He thought this might be the end of their new friendship with Owen. Too bad because they still needed his help. Besides, he was beginning to like Owen.

Owen quietly licked his blueberry popsicle.

Sam wondered what Owen was thinking. Would Abby and Sam see Owen tomorrow or had Abby ruined everything with her big mouth?

## Chapter Nineteen

"Wonder if Owen would like these chocolate chip pancakes," Abby said at breakfast the next day. "They're whole wheat and will give us energy for today. Just twenty-two more miles of lines to draw!"

*How could anyone be so energetic this early in the morning?* Sam wondered. "I'm a little sore from yesterday, but we gotta finish our project. There was no action on the Sleuth Cam last night. Guess whoever sabotaged the Paper Scrolls is staying away. Now they're locked up tight in the garage, so no worries."

"You always say 'No worries', Sam, but you worry enough for the whole family," Abby joked. "Lately we haven't seen Gordo, it hasn't rained in the barn, and we have Owen helping us. Life is good. Today is gonna be another great day. I can feel it!"

"Hope so, Abby." But Sam was thinking that after Owen questioned why we didn't wave to Joey, would he be back?

As Sam and Abby wheeled The Paper Scroll to the barn, he breathed a sigh of relief. Owen was riding up on his bike.

"Thanks for coming, Owen. You've really helped us," Sam said.

Owen smiled and said his usual, "Let's unroll!"

Abby smiled, feeling positive her good feelings about this day were coming true now that Owen was back.

Owen and Abby took their sides of the Paper Scroll while Sam knelt on the green foam gardening board.

"Oops," Abby said. Then she slid the cardboard under where Sam was

## CHAPTER NINETEEN

drawing.

Owen began to unroll the paper. . . "What is this, confetti? This wasn't there yesterday." He picked up a handful of what looked like crumbs.

Sam hurried over and examined the bits in Owen's hand. He said, "It can't be sabotage. They've been locked up tight in the garage overnight."

Abby bent down over the scroll. "Look, there's some little teeth marks on the edge of The Scroll."

Sam grabbed his phone. "Let me Google that!" He looked up and shook his head. "It says rodents like mice and rats will eat paper!"

Abby leaped up and said, "Ewwww! Rodents!"

Owen laughed.

Sam was staring at the bits of paper.

Owen said, "We get little field mice in our garage sometimes. Mom sets mouse traps for them. I'm the lucky one who has to empty the traps once the mice die in them."

"That's yucky!" Abby said.

Owen laughed.

"Well, I'm not gonna kill cute little mice," Abby said.

Sam made mice munching noises and stuck his teeth out.

Owen laughed again.

Abby glared at Sam. "This is serious. I'm not going to kill any animals."

"So," Sam said, "we're gonna make friends with them and just let them eat our Paper Scrolls? We're close to finishing our project and no mice are going to stop us"

"Chill, Sam. I have an idea," Owen said. "My aunt got one of those traps that doesn't kill mice. She puts peanut butter in the middle. When the mice go in the trap, slam! The door closes. Then she takes the mice outside and sets them free."

"Seems like a lot of work, and then the mice will just come back, laugh in our faces, and go back inside and keep munching on our Paper Scrolls," Sam said.

"I like Owen's plan, " Abby said . "Remember before Grandpa died, he had mice in his woodshed?"

"So?" Sam asked.

"So, he got those kinda traps like Owen's talking about. Wonder if Grandma still has them? We could set up a bunch of them and catch all those scroll-wreckers and take them far enough so they don't come back."

Owen nodded.

Sam tapped in a question on his phone. "I was afraid of that. It says you can't release them more than one hundred yards from where you caught them or they'll die."

"Why will they die?"

Sam sighed. "They won't be able to adapt to a new habitat."

"One hundred yards is almost the length of a football field," Owen said.

Abby smiled. "That should be far enough."

Sam said, "That's three hundred feet." He looked at Abby's hopeful face. "Okay, it's worth a try. After we finish the five lines today, we'll call on Grandma and see if she still has those traps." He shrugged his shoulders. "I can't believe I'm doing all this to save some mice because of my crazy sister."

Owen laughed.

Abby said, "Thanks, Sam."

"Can we now get to work?" Sam said, heading back to his post.

Taking turns being the pencil pusher made Sam's job easier. Changing positions relieved the strain on everyone's muscles.

Abby sharpened The Pencil four times.

Sam worried. The Pencil was getting tinier and tinier.

"My stomach's gurgling," Sam said just as their mother called them for lunch. They rolled up The Paper Scrolls and wheeled them back to the garage. "Only seventeen more miles to go if we can save our scrolls from these mice," he muttered.

Owen got on his bike.

Sam said, "Hey, aren't you staying for lunch?"

Owen smiled and stepped off the bike again.

Mom had set the table for all three of the hard workers.

"Yum" Owen said. "Mrs. J, this grilled cheese sandwich is delicious!"

Abby whispered, "It's swiss cheese and fresh tomatoes."

## CHAPTER NINETEEN

Sam said, "You don't have to whisper. I like it too. I even like the veggie dip."

Mom smiled and said, "Thanks, Owen. Let me know if you want more."

Sam was enjoying his meal and thinking about getting back to work when Abby decided to tell mom about the mice in the garage. Oh, no, he thought. Who wants to think about rodents when they're eating? He saw his mother put down her sandwich. Was she going to stop them from working because of the mice?

After listening to Abby telling the story, Mom said, "Let's call Grandma and see if she's still got those no-kill traps. We have to save your scrolls!"

Sam breathed a sigh of relief. He thought the worst was over.

# Chapter Twenty

Abby called Grandma.

Sam and Owen sat impatiently while Abby took what felt like an hour to tell Grandma every little detail about the rodents in the garage.

Abby finally hung up.

Sam asked, "So, what did Grandma say?"

Abby replied, "Grandma said, 'I don't like to get rid of things. You never know when you might need them. Come on over.'"

Abby and Sam headed for their bikes.

Owen said, "I guess I'll see you tomorrow."

Sam looked puzzled. "Hey, come with us. You'll meet Granny."

The three biked over to Grandma's house.

Sam saw Owen looked a little nervous, so he introduced Owen to Grandma.

Grandma Jackson smiled. "So you're the one helping The Mad Scientists! I heard about your clever idea of drawing five lines each day. Abby and Sam are lucky to have you for a friend."

Sam wished she hadn't called Owen a friend, but maybe he was.

Owen replied, "It's been fun. Or as my grandma would say, 'It's been a hoot.'"

Grandma Jackson asked, "Who is your grandma?"

"Thelma Parker. Do you know her?"

"Lordie! Why, we played bridge together for years, though I haven't seen her lately."

Owen sighed. "Grandma has her good days and her bad days. She gets out

## CHAPTER TWENTY

to the Senior Center when the bus picks her up or if we take her somewhere."

Grandma nodded and said, "Well, I'll call and see how she's doing."

Owen smiled. "She'd like that. We all need friends."

"You're a good one," Abby said. "He's been a big help, Grandma."

Sam only nodded.

Granny led them to the back door. "The traps are in the woodshed. Go on and get them. I have an old friend to call."

In the woodshed, Sam found three traps in the corner. He gave one to Owen and one to Abby. He thought she'd be afraid to touch it, being a girl, but she took it without a complaint.

Back at the house, Grandma said, "You can keep them. I really don't care if critters invade this old woodshed. I rarely go in there anymore."

"Thanks," Sam, Abby, and Owen said at once.

Owen said, "You did it again."

Sam laughed. "Hey, we're twins. But you said it too."

Owen said, "It's natural to say thank you. Isn't it?"

Sam smiled.

They each tied a trap to the back of their bikes and headed home.

Sam no longer worried about keeping up or being able to complete a ride. He liked riding his bike and feeling the breeze as he sped by the Gordon house.

Back home, Sam got a jar of peanut butter and a tablespoon. They each baited their traps and put them around the perimeter of the garage. "Well, I guess that's that," Sam said.

Owen said, "I wonder how far one hundred feet is from this garage?"

"We have to know that to keep our mice from dying," Abby said.

Sam glanced at his phone. "It's going to take time for us to walk and measure that distance. Dad doesn't have a tape measure that long."

Owen said, "There's a pedometer app that measures walking distance. Do you have it?"

Sam shook his head.

Owen pulled up his phone. "Mom got me this so she can check on Grandma and me when she's at work. Let me see if I can get the app."

Over ice pops, Abby and Sam watched Owen download the pedometer app onto his cell phone. "Got it," he said, showing his phone to Sam. "We're in business."

With purple, blue and orange lips and tongues, they set out from the garage walking.

Abby wondered where would the one hundred feet take them.

# Chapter Twenty One

The Three Mad Scientists walked straight from the garage across the backyard. Owen shouted, "Stop! We're at one hundred yards."

Sam looked. They were standing behind the barn.

Abby shook her head. "We can't release rodents near the barn."

Sam said, " Abby's right. Let's try going left from the garage and see where it gets us." He was growing impatient, worried the day would be done without them getting back to their task.

Back at the garage, Owen said, "Go!"

A hundred yards later, they were almost next door in the Mulvaney's backyard.

"I don't think the Mulvaneys would like us unloading mice in their yard, do you?" Abby asked.

The boys shook their heads.

"Back to the drawing board," Sam muttered as they headed back to the garage. This time, they went right until Owen said, "Stop."

That took them to the Jones's backyard.

"I don't think they'd appreciate mice jumping in their pool," Sam said.

Owen said, "Looks like we gotta drop 'em off as far back as we can behind the barn. What do you guys think?"

The twins agreed.

Sam said, "We'll have to check out the traps each morning 'til we're done with the project."

Abby nodded and said, "Let's unroll!"

"Hey, that's my line," Owen said and laughed.

Sam laughed too.

"Now let's see," said Owen. "Twenty-two miles left to draw. At five miles a day, that'd be four and a half more days. We could even shorten it to four days if we draw six lines in two days. That's twelve, then there'd be ten left to do in two more days."

"Way to go, Owen!" Abby said. "So tomorrow we can do six lines."

Sam nodded, "Thanks, Buddy." He looked funny. How did that slip out, he thought.

Owen stopped walking. "Ya know, Sam, I was gonna ask if you wanted Joey to help, too."

Sam got quiet. Here, it comes, he thought.

Owen continued, "I didn't know Joey bullied you, Sam. He's always been nice to me."

Sam tensed. "Yeah, maybe to you, but not to me. I tried ignoring Joey, but that didn't work. Once he started on me, he never let up."

Owen looked uncomfortable. "He likes to tease people—"

Sam snarled, "I need to get in his face and not back down."

Abby had been silent. "And I'll help. I've gotta protect my bro!" She looked at Sam. "You'd do that for me too. Wouldn't you, Sam?"

Sam realized he would. "No problemo, Sis!" He gave her a smile. "But you know, I have to do this myself. So, how about letting me stand up to Joey next time he starts in. OK?"

Abby nodded, feeling proud that Sam was finally ready to face his nemesis.

Owen looked anxious. "You know, I like you guys. But I've been friends with Joey a long time."

Sam nodded. "Owen, I like you too. I don't want to ruin your friendship with Joey." He found this difficult to say. "You were good pals with him first."

Owen glanced at the barn and said, "I'll still be friends with Joey but I want to finish this project with you." He smiled. "And I plan on telling Joey how much fun we had doing it. Besides, now you're both my friends, too."

Abby saw the relief on Sam's face.

Sam felt relaxed and smiled. "So, we'll see you tomorrow, right?"

Owen grinned. "As long as Grandma is feeling well, you can count on it."

CHAPTER TWENTY ONE

Abby watched Owen ride off and said, "Sam, I'm proud of you."
Sam replied, "You know, Abby, I'm proud of both of us."

# Chapter Twenty Two

Owen didn't show up the next day.

Sam was worried he might have changed his mind. Maybe Joey got to him.

Abby said, "He did say he might have to take care of his grandma. You have to admire him for that."

Sam nodded, but still wondered.

Without Owen, it was up to Sam and Abby to draw the six lines on the first Paper Scroll.

Sam checked the Sleuth Cam while Abby checked the traps in the garage. "Just some raccoons on the cam," he muttered. Then he heard Abby let out a screech.

Rushing into the garage, Sam saw Abby frozen in place, pointing to one of the traps. Inside was a cute little gray mouse with long whiskers.

"Is it dead?" Abby asked.

"Nope. Alive and kicking." Sam walked over to the other traps. One was empty and the third had a mouse that looked like the other one's twin. They looked more like twins than Sam and Abby did.

Sam saw Abby was staring at the mouse in the first trap. "It's only a little field mouse," he said. "Nothing to be afraid of." He thought of how Abby had helped him overcome his fear of Joey and wanted to help her with her fear of rodents. "You taught me not to be afraid of my bully, so you can get over your fear of these harmless critters too."

Abby's voice shook. "You're right. I'll take this trap if you'll take that one?" She took a deep breath and grabbed hold of the handle. "I'll risk all to save

## CHAPTER TWENTY TWO

the life of this creature."

"Don't worry," Sam said, "I'll release them if you don't want to."

They returned to the spot behind the barn which was full of tall trees. "It's a perfect place for these critters," Sam said. He stepped away from the trap and let the first little guy crawl out. He watched the mouse wiggle his nose and whiskers, look around, and then dash into the woods. "He was kind of cute," Sam said.

"It's show time," Abby said, forcing a brave smile holding the cage an arm's length away from her.

"You want me to do it?" Sam asked.

"No. I need to do this," Abby replied and cautiously pulled off the latch from the trap's door. She jumped back as the mouse raced from the trap into the grass. "I'm okay," she said. Sam started walking back, carrying the empty traps. "Let's put some more bait inside these traps and set them back in the garage."

Abby sniffed at her hands. "I want to wash my hands before we get ready to roll."

Sam waited until Abby returned, hoping Owen would show up. When he didn't, they wheeled The Paper Scrolls to the barn.

Abby hesitated unrolling the paper. Thankfully, no more confetti fell out. Maybe the plan was working, she thought, as she began to slide the paper over to where Sam was waiting. "This is gonna take all day without Owen," she said.

"Correcto," Sam said, getting on his knees. He took The Pencil, or what was left of it, out of his pocket. He wondered which was going to give up first, the pencil or Abby…or him?

It was a long, hot day. They only stopped for lunch and a few breaks to stretch and drink water. They switched off jobs about every hour or when one of them got tired or achy. Abby sharpened the pencil five times.

"Don't sharpen it too much, Abby, or it won't make it," Sam said, hoping this whole experiment didn't turn out to be a huge waste of time.

At four-thirty, Abby said, "Only sixteen more miles to go."

Sam groaned and said, "I hope Owen shows up tomorrow."

Abby was surprised but agreed.

After dinner, Sam yawned, "It's gonna be an early night for me."

Abby realized she'd been about to say the same thing.

As he tried to fall asleep, Sam saw a herd of sharp-teethed mice with rat faces chomping down on their huge rolls of paper. Behind them was a giant grinning face. Guess who?

## Chapter Twenty Three

At breakfast, Sam let out a loud yawn and said, "I sure hope Owen shows up today."

Abby replied, "I know he will. Wait and see."

Sam almost ran to the barn and shouted, "Hey, Owen, we missed you yesterday!"

Owen smiled and shouted, "Let's unroll!"

With Owen helping, they finished their work lickety-split, as Grandma says.

Sam was amazed at how having three of them working made the job go so much faster. He hoped Owen was really willing to accept being a part of what they now thought of as The Mad Scientist team. But each morning, he walked to the barn almost certain Owen would drop out. He was still afraid Joey would pressure Owen into dropping Abby and him as friends. He didn't mention Joey again. Instead he tried to make Owen feel as if he was an important member of the project.

Each day, Owen or Abby would announce the number of miles left to draw. It was ten, then five, and finally they were on the home stretch. Only five more miles to go.

Sam kept murmuring, "Hope the Pencil makes it. Hope the Pencil makes it." All that was left of it now was the eraser and a teeny-weeny stub of lead.

Each time they finished their day in the barn, Sam locked up the scrolls of paper and put the key under Germie's cage. Nothing was going to stop them now.

It was the last day. Owen and Abby were in the barn waiting for Sam.

Mom was waiting there, too, for the photo op. Suddenly, they heard screams coming from the house.

"That's Sam," Mom said.

Owen and Abby were already running. They couldn't make out what Sam was upset about until they got inside the house.

"Pencil! Pencil!" Sam kept screaming. "Where the heck is it?"

Dashing upstairs, Abby and Owen found Sam surrounded by dumped-out drawers on the floor. He kept repeating, "I put the pencil and the notebook away where I always keep them." He looked at Abby. "I've got the notebook. The pencil isn't in my pencil box."

Abby said, "Sam, calm down. I'm sure it's here somewhere. Have another look."

Owen said, "We'll all help you." "Thanks, Owen," Sam muttered. "I've looked everywhere." He looked at Abby, "If we can't find that pencil, we'll have to start all over."

The Mad Scientists tore the room apart. They moved the bed, took off the sheets, and shook them out. No pencil.

Abby crawled into Sam's closet and searched with a flashlight. "Yuck! Just smelly shoes and dust bunnies," she said, holding her nose.

Owen laughed. "You should smell my closet."

"No, thank you," Abby said.

While Sam went through every inch of his desk again, Owen crawled on his knees around the room. He used his hands to dig under the rug for the missing itty-bitty pencil stub. He even felt around inside Germie's cage. Still no pencil.

Finally, Sam sat on the rug. "I'm sorry, Abby. It's my fault. No pencil, no badge." He fought tears in his eyes. "After all the work we've done!"

Abby put her hand on Sam's arm to calm him down. "Let's ask Mom what she thinks. You've done your best." She looked at Owen. "We all have."

Wiping away a tear with his hand, Sam said, "You know Mom never helps us solve our problems. She says she wants us to be independent."

"Well, when she hears how hard we've tried, she'll want to help," Abby said.

"I wish I knew where that darn pencil went," Sam said.

## CHAPTER TWENTY THREE

Owen patted Sam's back. "It didn't just walk away. It'll show up."

Sam looked at Owen. Could he have taken it? He realized he was wrong to be suspicious still.

"Well, did you solve your problem?" Mom asked when they rushed into her art studio. She took one look at Sam and hugged him. "What's up? Whatever it is, it can't be that bad."

Abby told her about the missing pencil. "Ma, we really tried hard to solve this on our own, but it's gone."

"Without it, all our work was for nothing," Sam said.

Owen smiled. "Not for nothing," he said.

Mom looked at Sam. "It's got to be in your room or maybe in the barn."

"The barn!" They all shouted and ran toward the barn.

Sam was at the door first and yanked it open for the others. "How can it be here?" he asked, searching the floor.

Owen climbed up into the loft and used a flashlight to search every inch.

Sam used a rake on the floor while Abby held another flashlight searching the edges of the room.

No pencil.

"I don't get it," Sam said.

"I was about to say that," Abby muttered.

Owen's forehead wrinkled. "I've been thinking. Whenever I lose something, and that happens a lot, mom always asks me, 'What were you wearing yesterday?'"

Abby piped up, "Great! Sam, you were exhausted yesterday. Maybe you left it in your pocket?"

Sam tried to think. "Well, I wore my orange Jackson City Elementary School T-shirt… and blue shorts."

Owen asked, "Do your shorts have pockets?"

Sam shrugged. "I think so."

"Let's go," Abby said, and they were off and running again, this time, back to the house and the laundry room.

They dumped out the hamper and like squirrels searching for acorns, pulled at the laundry until Abby held up a pair of blue shorts and sang, "Ta da!"

Sam grabbed the shorts out of her hand, took a deep breath, and reached into the left pocket.

And there it was. The Pencil!

"Eureka!" Sam and Abby shouted and looked at each other.

"That's what I was going to say," Owen said. .

Sam looked at the tiny pencil and then at Owen. "I owe you big, Owen."

"Yes, you do," Abby said, giving Owen a wide smile.

Sam said,. "Now, without any more delays, let's see if this last surviving stub of a pencil can draw the last five miles."

## Chapter Twenty Four

The laundry room looked like it had been attacked by an angry flock of chickens, but the kids were smiling. They quickly put all the dirty clothes back into the hamper and with Sam proudly leading the way, paraded back to the barn. Sam led with the pencil held high in the air.

"Let's unroll," Owen said once they were back inside.

Abby said, "Sam, don't press down too hard. There's nothing left to sharpen."

Owen headed for his side of the barn and carefully unrolled the ball of paper.

Sam's hand shook while he drew the thirty-fifth line as the sheets of paper slid by him.

Abby's eyes were on The Pencil. Would it make it? After all this trouble, it was all up to a heroic stub of a pencil.

After a while, Sam got up, brushed off his knees, and shook out his arms and legs.

Owen asked, "Do you want me to take over?"

Sam said, "I can't believe it. We're finished!"

Abby jumped up. "Are you kidding us? We did it?"

Owen rose slowly. "Really, Sam?"

Sam nodded. "This little guy made it. We did it."

Abby and Owen raced over to admire what was left of The Pencil.

"We need a picture," Abby shouted and ran to get their mother, who took their picture holding one of The Scrolls and The Pencil. "Say, science badge," she said.

They all smiled and said, "Science badge!"

Owen was standing by the wall. He said, "You two are the real team," and started to walk away.

Sam grabbed his arm. "Hey, we never could have done this without our third Mad Scientist."

All three posed for more pictures.

Mom said, "Abby, I made your favorite, tuna and raisin sandwiches. Let's celebrate!"

Owen hesitated.

Sam leaned into his ear. "It's really pretty good."

Owen shook his head. "If you say so." He walked alongside Sam and Abby back to the house.

Abby saw Owen was examining the sandwich, as if afraid to taste it. "You don't know if you like something until you give it a try," she said.

"Someone," Sam said and bit into his sandwich.

Owen took a small bite. "Hey, not bad."

Popping open a bottle of lemonade, their mother said, "There's still a few weeks until school starts. Let's see what interesting facts we find this time. Hmmm. 'Every year, kids in North America spend half a billion dollars on chewing gum.'"

Abby said, "There's no badge for chewing gum."

Sam said, "Thank goodness."

Owen read his, "The average person laughs thirteen times a day."

Sam said, "Interesting, but there's no badge for laughing that I know of." He then read his lemonade lid. "Hmmm. Mine says, 'The average iceberg weighs 20,000 tons.' That's the weight of about 10 elephants." He looked at Abby. "How can we prove that one? With a gigantic underwater scale?"

They all laughed .

Finally Abby read hers, "'Smelling bananas can help you lose weight.' Sam, wanna prove that one?"

Sam said, "I'll sleep on it."

Mom laughed. "I wonder where you learned that?"

Abby and Sam both said, "Guess," and then looked at each other and burst into laughter. Sam studied his lid again. "You know, Abby, what makes you

## CHAPTER TWENTY FOUR

lose weight? Biking around Jackson City and then working in a super-hot barn all afternoon. I musta sweated off ten pounds, easy."

"You sure can ride your bike faster," Abby said.

Owen said, "Hey, Sam, how would you like to try out with me for the junior track team in September?"

Sam looked worried.

Abby shouted, "Sam, you'll be great."

"You'll like running and some of the other activities. We can be buddies," Owen said.

"Sure," Sam smiled and looked at Abby. "Looks like I reached my goal for the summer in more ways than one."

Abby said, "Let's go show Mr. and Mrs. Gordon the Pencil, the Paper Scrolls, and your Mad Scientist notebook. Then they can order our badges."

Sam said, "Owen, do you want to come with us?" Sam was thinking how Owen would feel if Joey was there.

"Sure," Owen said.

Loading everything into the wheelbarrow and pushing it across the street, Abby walked in front to keep The Scrolls from falling. Owen walked behind the wheelbarrow and kept an eye on The Scroll to make sure it didn't turn the barrow over on its side. Sam was walking next to him.

The closer they got to the Gordon house, the more nervous Sam became. He didn't want to ruin things between himself and Owen, his new friend.

Just as Sam feared, Joey was in the front yard. He saw Abby and then he saw Owen walking with Sam.

Sam was surprised Joey wasn't taunting him. He thought Joey's eyes were like burning coals, but he wasn't going to let even his worst enemy damage this day for him. "Hi, Joey," he said and walked past the stunned bully.

"Way to go, Bro," Abby whispered.

Owen waved, but Joey didn't wave back.

"You did the right thing," Owen said to Sam.

Sam nodded. He wondered if Joey would now leave him alone. He felt more confident. But he worried that one day he'd have to fight his bully.

Abby rang the doorbell.

Sam tensed. What if Mr. Gordon didn't accept his project? No, we worked too hard on this. He held the tiny pencil tighter.

# Afterward

Abby and Sam remembered their promise to their father and cleaned out the garage. The no-kill traps were still there. Abby laughed whenever she saw them.

The next day, Abby baked dozens of her oatmeal cookies for the Gordons, her Grandma, her parents, and for Owen Parker's family. She and Sam delivered them all and thanked everyone for helping them get their science and fitness badges.

Even Joey, seated with his parents and siblings, had to admit the cookies were some of the best he'd ever tasted. While he wasn't friendly with Sam, he didn't tease him. In fact, he seemed to be looking at Sam as if he'd never seen him before.

Later, Owen said, "I think Joey may lay off you from now on. He and I had a talk."

Sam wondered if even Owen could stop Joey from bullying him. He wasn't scared anymore but hoped Joey wouldn't force him into a fight. He didn't want Owen to have to choose whose side he'd be on.

When school started, Sam and Abby each wrote about "What I did Last Summer" for their classes. They actually had something exciting to write about. They wrote the stories about how they earned their Scout Badges and had learned to work together. Their teachers loved the stories and said it shows how hard work and determination can solve any problem. In other words, "Sleep on it."

When Mom and Dad got the assignments back, Mom sent their photos and essays into the Jackson City Times.

A few days later, Dad came rushing through the door while Owen and Sam were playing chess. "Guess what?! You made the front page!"

Owen beamed. The story mentioned Owen Parker's name, too, as a member of the Mad Scientist Club of Jackson City.

"I guess it's official," Abby said. "We are now the official Mad Scientist Club."

"So what do we do next?" Own asked.

Sam smiled. "We'll keep drinking lemonade and reading the facts in the lids until we find just the right math or science project for us to tackle next."

Owen raised his hand for a high-five. "Maybe, we can invite Joey to join?"

Sam slapped Owen's hand. "Maybe."

Abby thought, anything is possible.

## THE END

Will Joey Gordon leave Sam alone? Will Owen be able to stay friends with Sam and Abby while keeping Joey as his friend too? What new challenges will the Mad Scientists Club tackle next?

Find out in the next book from the Mad Scientist Club!

# Join the Mad Scientist Club

In *The Pencil That Wouldn't Die*, Sam and Abby started The Mad Scientist Club. Now's your chance to join!

Note: Get an adult's permission before continuing.

**Guessing and Measurement**

Abby and Sam travel a great distance around their neighborhood with their pencil. How far do you think Abby and Sam biked around their neighborhood over the summer? How far do you think you can travel around your neighborhood in a day? In a week? Follow the directions below to guess and check to see if you were right!

1. Just like Sam and Abby did, draw a map of your neighborhood. Show where your house is. Include the names of nearby streets and places important to you.
2. With an adult's supervision, plot a path around your neighborhood that you'd like to travel in one day. Guess how far you think walking, running, or biking this path will be. In the Guess the Distance chart on the next page, write your guess in the Guess column.
3. Walk, run, or bike your chosen path with an adult. Use a smart watch, fitness device, or smart phone app to help you measure the distance. Write down the distance on your Guess the Distance chart in the Actual column.

4. Repeat every day for a week, plotting a different path on your map and documenting your guess and actual distance in your Guess the Distance chart. Did your estimates get better each day?

# Guess the Distance

|  | Guess | Actual |
|---|---|---|
| Day 1 | _____ | _____ |
| Day 2 | _____ | _____ |
| Day 3 | _____ | _____ |
| Day 4 | _____ | _____ |
| Day 5 | _____ | _____ |
| Day 6 | _____ | _____ |
| Day 7 | _____ | _____ |

# Chart Your Progress

**Chart Your Progress**
Optional: Complete a Chart Your Progress bar graph to show the differences between your guesses and actual distances.

1. Find the difference (using subtraction) between your Guess and the Actual distance for Day 1.
2. Fill in the bar graph up to that number. (An example has been completed for you.)
3. Do the same for Days 2-7.

Now you have a visual showing whether your guesses got better each day!

# CHART YOUR PROGRESS

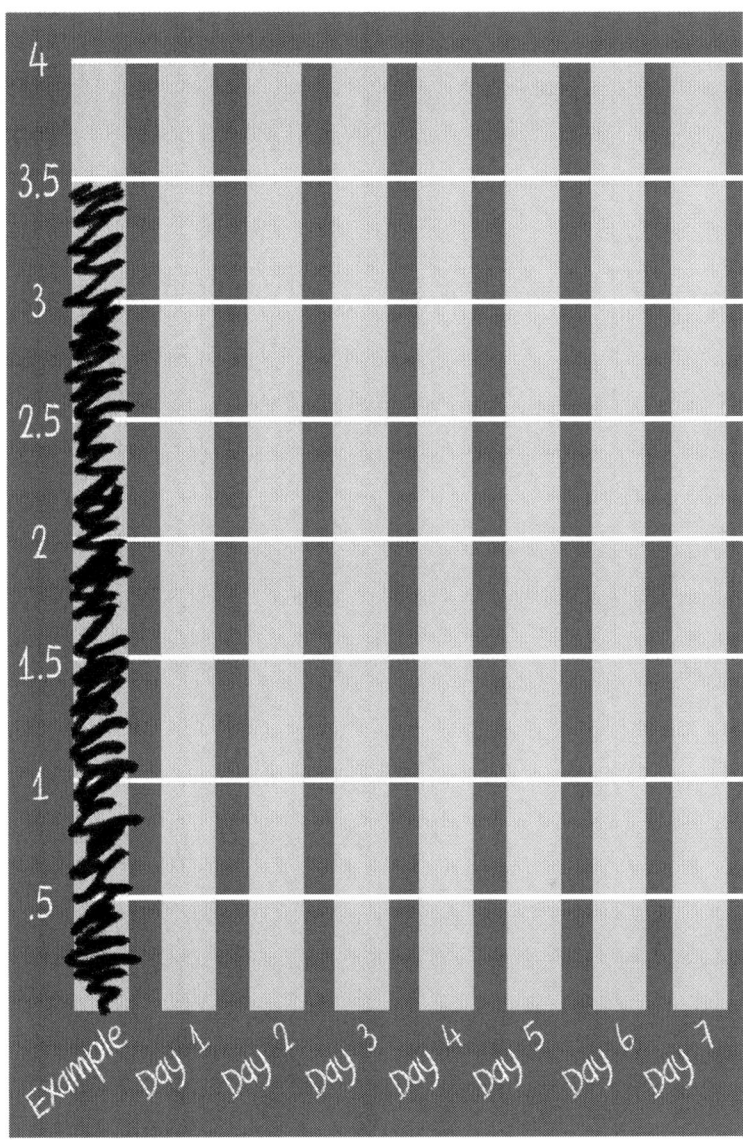

*Did your guesses get better as the week went on?*

# Coming Soon: The Case of the Lost Locket

# Chapter One

"Sam, come down here. You're not gonna' believe this," Abby called. Waiting for her twin brother, she was grinning like Whiskers, their well-fed cat.

"It's nine o'clock on Saturday. What's so important?" Sam asked, letting out a loud yawn.

"You need to sit down for this," Abby replied. She patted the sofa couch cushion next to her.

Sam plopped himself down and Whiskers jumped into his lap. "This better be good," he said stroking Whiskers.

"I just got a phone call from Emma Smith."

Sam's eyebrows shot up. "Emma called here?"

"She's in my class this year. She wanted to know if the Mad Scientist Club could help her solve a serious problem. I said I'd get back to her."

"Really?" Sam sat up straight, fully awake.

Fixing her green eyes on her twin's brown ones, Abby replied, "Really." She gave him a teasing look. "I know you kinda have a crush on Emma. Right?"

"Nah." He was embarrassed Abby had noticed. "So, what's her problem?"

It was Abby's turn to feel embarrassed. "You know, I didn't even ask her. She's coming over after lunch today. Do you want to call Owen so he can be at the meeting too? After all, he is a member of the Mad Scientists."

Sam hesitated. Owen was still good friends with Joey Gordon. Joey, aka Gordo, was the bully who plagued him for years. Thinking back at their last Mad Scientist project, he knew Abby felt they could trust Owen Parker, and they had invited him to be the third member of the Mad Scientist Club.

He still had some doubts but grabbed his cell phone and called. "Owen, are you busy after lunch today? It could be a new mystery for the Mad Scientist Club." He half-expected Owen to turn him down but smiled when Owen said, "Great. See ya' then." Relieved, he pocketed the phone, grabbed a whole wheat bagel and orange juice, and told his parents they had company coming.

Abby chimed in, "Yes, it's Emma Smith."

"Emma Smith? I know her mother from the PTA at Jackson Elementary School. Why's she coming over?" their mother asked.

Sam shot Abby a warning look and said, "I'll clean up outside, so we can meet on the front porch." He signaled Abby to follow him.

Sam was about to tell Abby not to say much until they knew what Emma wanted when Abby said, "I was thinking. Now that we're a club, why not have our meetings in the barn? It will be like a real clubhouse. I'll even make my killer oatmeal raisin cookies."

Sam nodded. "Works for me. Let's go."

The Jackson barn was a whirlwind of activity as they swept the floor and set up a corner for their clubhouse with four hay bales as seats. Tired and dusty, Abby suddenly poked her brother in the ribs, smiled, and said, "Hmmm? I wonder what Emma wants?"

Me, too, Sam thought.

# Chapter Two

Like most Saturdays, the Jacksons were eating lunch around the odd-shaped maple table that Grandpa Jackson built when there was a knock on the door.

When Sam opened it, he was disappointed. He saw Owen Parker's sandy mop of hair and not Emma's red curls. Forcing a smile, he high-fived Owen.

Owen slapped Sam's hand. "You don't look happy to see me, Sam. What's up?"

"I thought it was Emma Smith. She'll be here soon. She wants our help with something."

The Jackson tribe welcomed Owen like a long-lost member of the family. Grandma Jackson, aka Grandma J, asked about Owen's grandma.

Sam wasn't listening. His mind was on Emma and her "big problem."

The doorbell rang.

Abby hopped up and loped to the front door. More athletic than her twin, it was her natural stride that she used just before kicking a soccer goal.

A head full of red curls appeared, along with freckles, and gray eyes.

Sam's shoulders tightened.

Abby introduced Emma to everyone seated around the kitchen table.

Her mother smiled. "Emma, I know your mother from the PTA. How is she?"

Emma smiled. "Mom was fine when I left on my bike five minutes ago."

Sam liked Emma's sense of humor and laughed along with the others.

Mrs. Jackson said, "I've got lemonade, and Abby made her special cookies."

Clearing his throat, Sam quickly put in, "Ma, Owen, Abby wants the Mad

Scientist Club to meet in the barn. Okay?" Smile, he told himself, feeling Emma's eyes turn to him.

"Sure," Owen said.

Mrs. Jackson nodded. "Help yourselves then."

They each took a chilled bottle of lemonade, and Abby carried the cookies.

Sam pulled open the barn door and turned to Emma. "This is our Mad Scientist Clubhouse."

"Cool," Owen said, sitting on a hay bale.

Abby offered Emma a cookie.

"Thank you, Abby," Emma said and sat on the bale opposite Sam.

Abby started the conversation. She welcomed Emma to make her feel comfortable. "You know our third MSC member, Owen, right?"

"Since there are only two classes for each grade at Jackson Elementary, I have a fifty percent chance of being in a class with any of you." She smiled at Owen. "Hi, Owen."

Owen nodded, busy chomping down his cookie.

Sam cleared his throat and aimed his eyes at Emma, "Did you read about the Mad Scientist Club in the paper?"

"Yes," Emma said. "It sounds like you three had fun." She looked serious. "They made it sound like you solved mysteries—"

Owen said, "The reporter called it the case of The Pencil that Wouldn't Die."

Sam added, "We were proving that a pencil can draw a line thirty-five miles long."

"And we got scout badges, too," Abby said. Holding up her lemonade bottle, she began to tell the whole story: "It all started when we opened our lemonade bottles last summer and read the fun facts on the lid. The pencil fact was in Sam's lid—"

"Abby, she read the newspaper story," Sam interrupted.

Owen leaned forward and took another cookie. "Yum, Abby. I don't know how you get them crispy on the outside and soft in the middle. Anyway, Emma. I didn't join up with the twins early on." He sighed. "Now that my parents are divorced, my mom is back to work, and sometimes I have to stay with my grandma...take care of her."

## CHAPTER TWO

Clicking lemonade bottles, Sam said, "But once Owen came on board, he worked as hard as we did. And he showed up at the barn most days. By the end of the project, we asked him to become a member of The Mad Scientist Club." He gave Owen a big smile.

"Err…" Emma hesitated, her eyes looking worried. "That's why I'm here. To ask you for help."

Sam, Abby, and Owen leaned forward, waiting for Emma to finally tell them about her problem.

Sam saw the sad expression appear on Emma's face. Why did Emma Smith need their help?

# Chapter Three

A hush fell over the group. All eyes were on Emma Smith.

*Well?* Sam thought. "Emma, what's wrong?"

Owen leaned forward even more.

Abby studied Emma's eyes.

It seemed like forever, but at last, Emma spoke, "I was very close with my Gram… my father's mother. She died last year." Looking as if she were almost in tears, Emma continued, "Gram wore a silver locket around her neck… until she gave it to me two years ago, for my eighth birthday. It was on a silver chain. Gram wore it when she came here from Ireland with Grandpa." She hesitated. "I put a small picture of the two of us in the locket, and on the other side, there was a photo of my cat, Fluffo."

"Is she big like Whiskers?" Owen asked.

Emma smiled slightly. "She's even bigger."

"Go on with your story," Sam said, shooting Owen a look for interrupting.

Emma nodded. "Anyway, I wore the locket for two years. I took it off when I practiced gymnastics. Our coach said not to wear necklaces cause we might choke."

"That makes sense," Abby said.

Emma glanced at Abby and continued, "I took it off, and I thought I put it on the top shelf in my room, but it's not there. I've searched my room, even moved my bed, but can't find it—"

"Are you sure it was on the top shelf? Could it be somewhere else?" Abby asked.

Emma shrugged. "That's the last place I remember putting it. But now, I'm

## CHAPTER THREE

not so sure."

Sam was busy taking notes on a half-used spiral notebook.

Owen rubbed his chin, still leaning forward. "So far, we know that you lost your silver locket about two weeks ago," he said.

"And that the last place you remember seeing it was on the top shelf in your room," Sam added.

Digging into her handbag, Emma said, "Yes. I almost forgot. I brought a photo of Gram wearing the locket…before she gave it to me." She handed the photo to Abby, who examined it and then handed it to Sam, who then gave it to Owen.

Owen peered at the photograph with a magnifying glass he'd begun to carry with him since joining the MSC. "It looks like a locket, all right," he muttered.

"Ya know, Emma," Abby said, "I read a lot of mysteries. So, I'm wondering why you'd even put your locket on that shelf."

Emma laughed. "You don't live in my house with Brady and Luke. Brady's eight and Luke's six, and they get into all kinds of mischief. I've caught them snooping around my room when they thought I wasn't around. So I put it up high where they can't reach it."

Sam stopped writing and aimed his eyes at Emma. "Have you asked your brothers about taking the locket?"

Abby added, "Or if they've seen it?"

Emma shook her head. "No. Because then they'd tell Mom and Dad." She bit her lip. "I've been trying to find it myself. So I don't have to tell my parents." Emma wiped away a tear.

Abby looked at Sam.

Sam reviewed his notes and said, "So far, we have Luke and Brady as suspects." He peered into Emma's eyes again. "Before we can do anything, you need to snoop around their rooms, to see if the locket is there—"

"So, the Mad Scientists Club agrees to help Emma?" Owen asked, a proud smile on his face.

Sam and Abby nodded and said at the same time, "Yes."

Sam stood and held up his fist.

Abby and Owen joined Sam and fist-bumped each other.

"Looks like we're all in." Abby smiled. "We're going to help you, Emma."

Emma stood. "Thank you. It might take a couple of days for me to check out their rooms. I'll call Abby when it's time for you guys to come over. Okay?"

"Good," Abby replied. "That will give us time to plan our next moves."

"I feel a little better already. Thanks a lot," Emma said as she hopped on her bike parked outside the barn.

Sam noticed Emma's dimples as she smiled.

As she rode off on her bike, Emma gave the three detectives a wave.

"We've got another case," Owen exclaimed.

"She's in real trouble," Abby said. "I hope we can help her."

Sam nodded. "I guess we'll have to wait and see."

## YOU WON'T HAVE TO WAIT LONG FOR THE NEXT EXCITING MYSTERY WITH THE MAD SCIENTISTS CLUB: THE CASE OF THE LOST LOCKET

Sign up for the NCG Narrative at newhousecreativegroup.com to be among the first to find out more about The Case of the Lost Locket and the rest of the Newhouse Creative Group family of authors.

# Subscribe to the NCG Narrative

**FREE Book for Subscribing to The NCG Narrative**

Subscribe to our free newsletter, **The NCG Narrative**, to immediately receive a **FREE** eBook from Newhouse Creative Group.

Be the first to learn about NCG's newest releases, get behind the scenes of NCG, enter NCG Narrative exclusive contests and giveaways, and much more!

Subscribe today at NewhouseCreativeGroup.com

# More from AimHi Press and Newhouse Creative Group

Visit AimHiPress.com for more books and other products from AimHi Press and the rest of the Newhouse Creative Group family!

# About the Author

Growing up an identical twin in western Pennsylvania influenced Sharon's early years. The Carnegie Free Library was her favorite place to get books and go to Story Hour each Friday with her sister. Libraries and books are still vital for Sharon's daily existence. The author of eight books for children, the genres range from science plays to picture book fiction and biographies, to middle grade and teen novels. "I look for ideas everywhere I go and they seem to fall in my lap," Sharon said.

Sharon's latest book, The Pencil That Wouldn't Die, is the first of the Mad Scientist Club books for middle grade children. What starts out as a summer scout project for twins Abby and Sam Jackson, becomes an adventure. They learn a lot along the way and make big changes in themselves. Sam and Abby are looking for another Mad Scientist adventure right now!

You can learn more about Sharon and her books on her website sharonsbooks.net and at newhousecreativegroup.com.

**You can connect with me on:**

- http://www.sharonsbooks.net
- http://www.newhousecreativegroup.com

# Also by Sharon K Solomon

**A Walk with Grandma (Newhouse Creative Group)**
A delightful picture book for all ages. Alex and his grandma walk through the city as Alex teaches her a fun game. A wonderful way to teach the animal-vegetable-mineral game to children. Sequel to the award-winning, A Walk with Grandpa.

**A Walk with Grandpa (Raven Tree)**
Beautiful illustrations as Daniella and her grandpa take a walk in the woods and play a special word game.

**Primary Science Readers Theatre (Pieces of Learning)**
Funny science plays that elementary school students and teachers will enjoy acting or reading out loud.

**Cathy Williams, Buffalo Soldier (Pelican Publishing)**
Picture book biography of the only documented female Buffalo soldier. The fascinating story of Cathy, who disguised herself as a man and joined the U S Army after the Civil War.

**Christopher Newport, Jamestown Explorer (Pelican Publishing)**
Picture book biography of the British Explorer who discovered and established the colony of Jamestown, Virginia.

**Lewis Tewanima, Born to Run (Pelican Publishing)**
Picture book biography of the inspring Hopi Olympic medal winner.

**Ride High with the Wave (The Gettier Group)**
Middle grade chapter book about two swim team rivals with a mutual problem. Can they work together to solve it?

**James Smith, Four Years a Mohawk (Amazon)**
Teen historical fiction novel about James Smith's adventurous life with the Mohawks during the French and Indian War.

Made in United States
Orlando, FL
02 March 2022

15264453R00065